State of California

EDMUND G. BROWN JR.
GOVERNOR

February 12, 1976

Dear Frank:

I share your concern that so little attention has been given to the Spanish and Mexican heritage of California. As we recall the achievements of Jefferson and Franklin and the other founding fathers in this bicentennial year, we should not ignore the contributions of De Anza, the Franciscans, and those bold explorers who pioneered California. They are our "founding fathers".

Your efforts to remind Californians of their heritage is an example of what the bicentennial should be about.

Sincerely,

EDMUND G. BROWN JR.
Governor

De Anza's Trail Today

by

FRANK RILEY

The drama of the Anza Expedition that
founded San Francisco in 1776;

A guide to fascinating discoveries
along the Anza Trail in 1976

Photography by Frank & Elfriede Riley

a WORLD WAY publication

Published by WorldWay Publishing Company and WorldWay West

Worldway Postal Station,
P.O. Box 92705
Los Angeles, California 90009

Printed in the United States of America

Acknowledgements:

To Los Angeles Magazine, which published an article based on this book in January 1976;

To the Los Angeles Times, San Francisco Examiner & Chronicle, Denver Post and Chicago Tribune which have published Frank Riley's syndicated columns containing portions of this material;

To Saturday Review and Carte Blanche magazines which have published articles by Frank Riley with additional background data used in this book;

To Helen Shropshire and the California Heritage Guides, coordinators of the Re-Enactment of the De Anza Expedition for California committees—and to Kenneth McClure and the Arizona Bicentennial-International Anza Bicentennial Committee—for invaluable historical data, maps, photographs;

To Barbara Durham, University of California at Berkeley Press, for permission to use material from the source books of all Anza historical data: The 5-volume series *Anza's California Expeditions* by the late Professor Herbert Eugene Bolton, published in 1930 by The Regents of the University of California.

Cover design—and updating and adapting of maps—by Hector Delgadillo. Typography by Austerity Type, Inc. Printed by Donahue Printing.

Contents

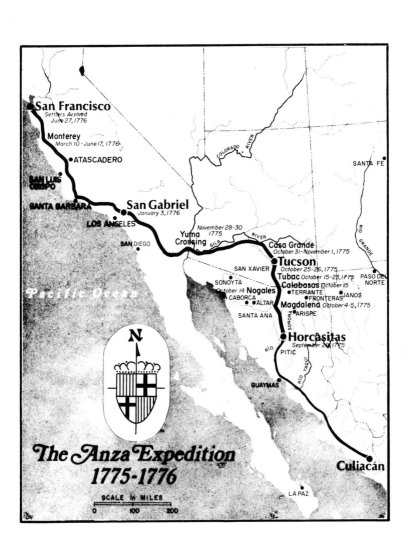

The Anza Expedition
1775-1776

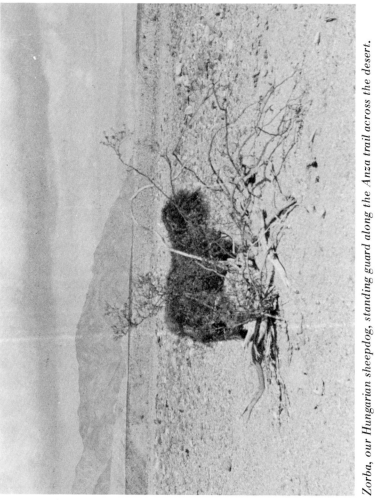

Zorba, our Hungarian sheepdog, standing guard along the Anza trail across the desert.

I.

In the hoofprints of history

For some 800 miles by bicycle and afoot, my wife Elfriede and I have been traveling between the Mexican border and San Francisco—following a trail lost to most travelers for nearly two centuries.

This is the route of the pioneering Anza expedition of 1775-76, which brought 240 colonists from Mexico across the parched deserts, then over the southern Sierras during the worst winter ever recorded to found the city of San Francisco. It is California's own Bicentennial event.

Historically, the Anza trail is delineated more clearly than any other trail that opened the West. This is due to the remarkable diaries of Juan Bautista de Anza and the expedition's official chaplain—scholarly, ascerbic Father Font. Two great California historians, Hubert Howe Bancroft and Herbert Eugene Bolton—especially Bolton, spent decades of their lives researching and recreating that epochal era. Of more general interest, the well-written and thoughtful book by Richard F. Pourade, *Anza Conquers the Desert*, was published in 1971. Yet not one in ten thousand travelers who drive along or close to the route every week of the year has any awareness of following in the hoofprints of history. Only a few widely scattered and mostly isolated historical monuments mark particular places along the trail. They have been known principally to small groups of equestrians who over the years would ride parts of the route closest to their own communities.

Tracing and retracing the entire route in the autumn of 1975, we wanted to find out if the Anza trail still could fascinate contemporary travelers in California, during and after the Bicentennial year. We found it to be an overwhelming sensory and learning experience. We discovered how little we really knew about California, how shallow is the depth of much of California history taught our children. Continually we would come upon magic places and experiences not encountered before during our previous six years of non-motorized explorations up and down the coast, valleys and mountains of the state:

Sunsets like mellow gold on a California lake we never knew existed. . . .

A positively pastoral way across the entire Los Angeles basin, without even the murmur of freeway traffic. . . .

A desert-to-mountains pass that has been traveled for 200 years, but has never been covered with pavement—or even declared to be a road. . . .

The haunting beauty of Point Conception seen not from the sea but from the land, where there has been no road in this century. . . .

Wild humming birds so unafraid of the human presence that they hung suspended beside the petals of a late autumn flower, while I edged carefully by on a narrow path. . . .

Superb restaurants and inns tucked away where we didn't suspect they could survive. . . .

The world's first motel and the world's most rococo motel thriving in the same central California community. . . .

Another Hearst castle, this one long forgotten despite its Byzantine gilt dome, appearing as a total surprise on a hill near Jolon, a once mainstream and pleasantly sinful community turned into a ghost town by a military reservation. . . .

2

The waterman of Casmalia who inherited the town's water concession from his father, and who sleeps with his wife in the bedroom in which he was born. . . .

A Franciscan mission priest who could—with a small but eloquent shrug—forgive Governor Jerry Brown for not supporting a California Bicentennial: "After all, he was trained by the Jesuits—and that tells you something, doesn't it?"

These memories linger, along with others that make us laugh, angry and sad.

The Anza trail today is definitely one you will want to follow in your own path of discovery and rediscovery. Hopefully, you will be able to bike or walk at least parts of it. But if time or health make this impractical or unwise, you can drive rather close to all but two sections of the actual route. And one of these can be viewed splendidly from the picture window of an Amtrak train. You can even, as the Committee for the Re-enactment of the De Anza Expedition has demonstrated, follow the trail in the saddle of a horse.

Do make an effort, though, to do some walking or bicycling. Walking will bring you most in harmony with the countryside as the Anza pioneers saw it; some parents had to carry small children as they trudged along.

Not until you bike or walk along a country road, and cringe at the sound and smell of a car roaring past, do you realize fully what price the now tottering god of the automobile has made you pay for being a micro part of the most mobile society on earth. Deadening of the senses may be the highest price of all.

Everything, from enchantment to anger, is intensified when you slow down the pace of travel. Each view is seen for a long time, as in slow motion. Wild flowers open for you in the morning and close in the evening. The wind and surf are orchestrations. There is time to touch other lives more intimately, to give and receive a wave, a smile.

Every roadside, even this late in the 20th century, teems with small life you never knew was there. When you stop for a bite of lunch out of your pack, a lizard, gopher, squirrel and sometimes a rabbit will take turns checking you out. Horses are indifferent to you, dogs dislike you, cows invariably adore you. A herd will turn its heads as one to stare wide-eyed and unblinking as you pass by. Deer finally run, but not urgently.

Off-freeway towns are rich in collector's items. If you collect railroad stations, those around Oceano and Lompoc are gems from a vanished era. They're painted a deliciously atrocious mustard color, as if the railroad had once been offered a bargain in paint and bought enough to last half a bicentennial.

Anger is especially intensified. Anger at developers, road-builders and assorted private property interests that actually have closed off to the public one of the most scenic sections of what should be preserved for all time as an historic trail.

If you drive parts of the Anza trail in your car, drive slowly enough to wave now and then at a fellow traveler; that kind of wave is fast disappearing from our culture.

Along the way, you will often encounter the over-lapping trail of the Committee for the Re-enactment of the De Anza Expedition. We'd never heard of this volunteer group when we started out on our own trek, but soon we began to meet interesting and committed people who responded at once to what we were trying to do, and who let us share some of their dreams and frustrations. The idea for the California committee was germinated in Monterey in 1973 by Helen Shropshire, a gracious lady who donates her time to the California Heritage Guides around the Monterey Peninsula. She involved her film-maker husband, and they flew their own plane thousands of miles to coordinate the re-enactment in California with what would happen earlier in Mexico and Arizona. They had to deal with problems Anza never faced: "Like you can't bring

4

200 horseback riders into a town and ask to use the john at a Texaco station . . . and how about the horses?"

Southern California riders from Imperial, then San Diego and Riverside Counties, took over from their Arizona counterparts after the Colorado River crossing in Yuma. Young people waded the chill waters to recreate what men, women and children in the Anza party faced 200 years earlier. Another group of riders left San Gabriel Mission in the east Los Angeles area and trekked on across the San Fernando Valley, dressed in costumes of the Anza period. Similar groups were ready to carry on from community to community, observing the timetable of California's first pioneer families—who reached Monterey on March 6, and San Francisco on June 10, 1776.

The riders and the festivals dramatically focussed attention on one of the world's most neglected historic trails. It is our own hope that by charting the route for walkers, bikers and all the other travelers who don't ride a horse, it will become an ongoing part of the California experience and not be forgotten after the Bicentennial year has passed into history.

We don't mean to put down the other Bicentennial events in California, all carried out through volunteer efforts—a striving to say and do something meaningful about a revolution that is still ongoing in so many ways after 200 years.

But for the historic parallel between the founding of a new nation and the colonizing of a future state simultaneously on the east and west coasts of a vast continent, the 240 colonists who braved the overland trail into California from the mainland of Mexico were in the same time frame with what was happening in Boston and Philadelphia. The Gold Rush was officially designated as the centerpiece of California Bicentennial festivals, though in fact the Gold Rush drew into the Mother Lode some of the great-grandchildren of the Anza pioneers who had founded San Francisco. A lack of apparent relevance

5

between 1849 and 1776 prompted Governor Jerry Brown—soon after taking office—to slam the till on state spending for the Bicentennial. He told associates, "The Bicentennial has nothing to do with California—let's get on with today's problems."

I know Jerry Brown as a sensitive and perceptive person. I don't believe he would feel quite the same if he could find time to bike or walk part of the Anza trail with us—or if he could meet Brother Timothy of Mission San Antonio near King City, who came up with the idea of riding a donkey with the Anza horsemen and women traveling from his mission to Monterey. Don't dismiss Brother Timothy as simply a pious country friar—although his isolated mission is in a part of California that would not look greatly changed to Juan Bautista de Anza. An urbane scholar and historian, Brother Timothy greeted us in slacks and sportshirt when we arrived at Mission San Antonio. He said, as we talked in the old book-panelled library: "After what this country has gone through the last few years, the Bicentennial year is a good time for each of us to make some kind of re-commitment."

Without belaboring the point, our biking and hiking along some 800 miles of the Anza trail was—in addition to all else—also something of a small personal pilgrimage. We had been turned on to the Bicentennial a couple of years earlier while visiting in Hawaii, where we became involved with the Polynesian Voyaging Society. This group, as Hawaii's contribution to the Bicentennial year, was preparing to sail 2,000 miles of open ocean to Tahiti in a replica of the canoe that brought their ancestors to Hawaii. "This would be a great thing for Hawaiian people," Herbert Kawainui Kane—architect, artist and skipper of the canoe, told us. "It could give us a new sense of pride. If we survive the voyage, it will prove that our ancestors came here as skilled navigators—not as lost drifters on the winds and currents of chance."

6 California's Mexican-American people, looking back

across nearly two centuries of second class citizenship to the expedition of Juan Bautista de Anza, can share this same feeling of pride. The era of the American revolution was never strictly WASP.

II.

What the Anza Expedition was all about

It's difficult to keep our own history in perspective during a Bicentennial year, but on the eve of the American Revolution much of the Old World was facing change; waves from across the Atlantic and Pacific rolled upon the shores of a New World already old.

Spain had dominated Mexico and the Pacific Coast for more than a bicentennial, and an empire scarcely perceived was in ebbtide. To Carlos III of Spain, this empire faced multiple threats. English-speaking frontiersmen were looking at his Louisiana border. The Russians were looking at the California coast in a calculating way. A hostile Indian frontier, reaching from the Gulf of Mexico to the Gulf of California, was as long as the Rhine-Danube line that had once over-extended the Roman Empire. Somewhere to the north, the legendary River of the West was still believed to exist; the French and English had only to discover it in order to find easy access to the Pacific.

Spain had long considered and tentatively explored the possibility of its own easy access from the mainland of Old Mexico to the coast of Alta California. San Diego harbor had been known since 1542. Vizcaino had renamed the bay of San Diego and studied the Bay of Monterey in 1601 and 1602, yet Manilla galleons plying the Pacific still had to carry cargo far down the coast of the South Sea to Acapulco. As early as 1540, Melchoir Diaz had led an

8

expedition across the Sonoran desert in northwest Mexico, only to be turned back by what he described as the boiling mud of the Colorado River delta. And while beginning the settlement of New Mexico in 1548, Juan de Onate probed to the Colorado River far to the north of its delta, and on the distant horizon could discern what would come to be known as the San Bernardinos of the Tranverse Range. As the 17th century was ending, Jesuits began stretching mission outposts up Baja California.

To discourage Russian interest in the harbors of Alta California, Carlos III directed Portola and Father Junipero Serra to establish missions at San Diego and Monterey. The Franciscans and Serra had long preempted the Jesuits. Portola had already traveled up the coast by land and sea. But the sea route was precarious, and Baja California couldn't sustain a population base to support a colonial outreach that would be more than a symbol of possession.

In 1774, Captain Juan Bautista de Anza, age 36, was commander of a small frontier post at Tubac, in what is now southern Arizona. A Captain in the King's army, he was also a son of Mexico; his father had been born in Mexico and had died fighting Indians on this same frontier. Anza was Spanish in the same sense that George Washington, at age 36, was British.

In boyhood, Anza had dreamed of pioneering an overland route to the Alta California coast. As a frontier captain, he talked with enough Indians and wandering padres to disbelieve the prevailing concept that not one but two impassable ranges walled off the coast from the searing desert. Colorado River Indians could draw pictures of the coastal ships; they knew when Portola was proceeding by land up the coast, only a few days to the west. Franciscan Father Garcés, a man of incredible courage, wandered alone beyond the frontier outposts and into what would someday be Imperial Valley. He wrote on September 29, 1771: "I was perplexed on the 29th over what direction I should take in a place so scant of water. I   9 feared to go to the west because it appeared to me that I would not encounter the river. Neither did it seem well to go to the sierra by northwest or north, in spite of the fact that I saw two openings. . . ."

Anza became convinced there was only one range, and that it was breached by at least two passes. He got permission to prove his point by leading a small exploratory expedition that left Tubac on January 9, 1774—a few days after the Boston tea party. On maps of North America then extant in the Thirteen Colonies, the future state of California was named New Albion, a vague territory bounded on the north by the mythical River of the West.

Anza went across the desert, over the Sierras and on to the Mission at Monterey, a feat comparable to what Lewis and Clark accomplished thirty years later. Lewis and Clark got all the ink in history books, but if they had then returned to Missouri and made a second trip with 240 colonists in tow, their place in history would have been more comparable to Anza's—providing they had been able to lead their settlers through the worst winter ever recorded in the southern Sierras, and with the loss of only one life, a young mother in childbirth.

Bucareli, Viceroy of Mexico and spokesman for Carlos III, had supported Anza's first expedition, and now backed his proposal to found the city of San Francisco. Anza wrote to Bucareli in Mexico City on November 17, 1774: "Complying with what your Excellency is pleased to order me with regard to the forty families who might go with me to occupy the River of San Francisco, let me say that the people whom I consider best suited for the purpose and most easy to get without causing a lack in their country, at the same time that the individuals sought may be benefited, are those of the alcaldías of Culiacán Sinaloa and Fuerte, in the province of Sonora. Most of their inhabitants I have just seen submerged in the direst poverty and misery, and so I have no doubt they would most willingly and gladly embrace the advantages which your Excellency may deign to offer them." Diplomatically but firmly, Anza spelled out what he wanted: "If your Excellency should be pleased to approve this plan, it will be very important that the necessary effects be sent without loss of time, so that they may be at Culiacán or Sinaloa in the month of next March, in order that when I arrive there in the same month I may supervise their distribution among the recruits whom I shall then begin to raise, and who, I beg to tell your Excellency, both themselves as well as their families, will have to be equipped from shoes to hair ribbons." Anza, a methodical genius for detail, had already decided not to distribute cash, which might promote "gambling and prodigality."

Culicán had celebrated its own centennial before the founding of Boston. Now the boom days of silver mining were gone. Life was hard, and California did sound like the promised land. Particularly when Anza showed up not only with shoes and hair ribbons, but with white petticoats, Brussels stockings, leather jackets.

There were saddle horses but no covered wagons on this trek to a new land; the prairie schooners came along after Anza had proved that women and children could survive a crossing of desert and mountains. His families were picked for sturdiness of body and mind, good temper and adventurous spirit. Most had from four to nine children; fathers would be expected to carry the smallest offspring. Supplies would be on pack animals, and would have to be loaded and unloaded daily. Nights, in desert or snow, would be spent in tents. There would be nearly a thousand horses, pack animals, beef cattle. Anza added three barrels of brandy to such other basics as sixty bushels of beans and thirty loads of flour for tortillas. The brandy was to become a continuing source of irritation to Father Font, selected as the official chaplain.

Fray Pedro Font was a least likely as well as a most inspired choice. He could be imperious, aloof, quarrelsome, and also capable of great self-sacrifice. He had the eye and the ear of a novelist. When irritated with his Commander, he would write of the cross a man of God had to bear in getting along with "these absolute lords." And he could never entirely submerge the attitude that his Commander was after all a Mexican colonial, while he himself was a gentleman of Spain, a Catelonian—educated as a geographer, mathematician, musician. For the previous ten years after coming to the New World, his assignment had been not a Mission among Indians, but as scholar and teacher at the College of Santa Cruz de Querétaro. Anza had selected him because of his ability to take position sightings from the stars. Adding to the drama inherent in their different backgrounds and personalities, Father Font was not in rugged health. He suffered from recurring malaria, which often made him less than patient with the "absolute lord" under whom he was fated to serve. He was also precise about the need to say Mass every morning, and sometimes the Mass would go on and on while he delivered a sermon aimed at the fandango of the previous night, and while his Commander fumed to get under way. The contrapuntal roles of Anza and Font, and that of the widow who was so often to scandalize her austere Chaplain, were the stuff of uncontrived drama.

For Anza, the logistics of getting his expedition under way each morning was like setting a small city in motion. The route through northwestern Mexico to Tubac was the ancient Road to Cibola, the Camino Real which for centuries had linked mines, missions, ranchos, thriving towns and frontier forts with the splendors of Guadalajara and Mexico City. At Horcasitas, Anza learned that the fiercely independent Apaches—warriors from the same tribe that had killed his father—had raided Tubac and made off with 500 horses being held for the expedition. Reluctantly, he had to use his imperial authority to begin commandeering more horses. Tubac was still 200 miles away.

The expedition was ready to leave from Tubac, where Anza and his father and grandfather had served, on the morning of October 22, 1775. Father Font said a Mass for its success. You can almost feel him rolling over his own words on his tongue as he later recorded them for posterity in his diary. Moving on from the gospel, he went into a sermon "comparing the journey of the children of Israel through the Red Sea to the promised land with the journey of the present expedition across the Colorado River to Monterey." He promised the protection of the Virgin of Guadalupe, but warned sternly of the wrath of God in the case of any misconduct along the way. In his summation, he reprised the rewards of virtue in this earthly life, then detailed the joys of eternal rest that would await the deserving in the future beyond the grave. Finally, Anza was able to give the order to mount.

A soldier's wife died in childbirth that first night. Father Font went to her tent to pray with her and give comfort to the husband. It was to be the only loss along the way. Friends cared for the child, and it became one of the first citizens of San Francisco.

(*Author's Note:* The parallel stories of the Anza Expedition of 1776—and our efforts to retrace the trail for the contemporary traveler—will now be told on facing pages, respectively marked by the symbol from Anza's shield and the outline of a bicycle.)

It was late in November when the colonists reached the Colorado River, in the strong nation of the Yuma Indians. Chief Palma, a friend of Anza's from the exploratory trip of 1774, rode out to greet them. His people brought gifts of grain, fruit, vegetables—including watermelons.

Anza, Father Font and others of the expedition staff were housed in a lodge especially built for them. They were received by Palma's wife and family. While his people were being made comfortable, Anza searched out a new ford near the present city of Yuma. Father Garcés, the wandering padre, had come this far to stay among the Yumas until Anza's return from San Francisco. He was ill, and Font wrote:

"Father Garcés was carried across the river on the shoulders of three Yumas, two at his head and one at his feet, lying stretched out and face up as though dead. I crossed over on horseback, and since I was ill and dizzy headed, three naked Indians accompanied me, one in front guiding the horse, and one on each side holding me in order that I might not fall. Since our expedition stretched out so long, we spent about three hours fording the river, and in order to dry things out that got wet we halted on its very bank. . . ."

They camped on the night of December 4, 1775, below a hill called Cerro de San Pablo, now Pilot Knob, which helped narrow the channel of the Colorado River as it rushed southward.

14

III.
Mexican Border to Borrego

In the cool of twilight on Sunday, November 30, 1975, we visited a small party of horsemen around their campfire near Pilot Knob in California's Imperial County, just west of Yuma and close to the All-American Canal. They had taken over in mid-afternoon at the Colorado River from the Arizona committee for the Anza expedition re-enactment, which had organized groups of riders to travel sections of the Anza trail all the way up from Sonora.

The horsemen around the campfire were citizen members of the Sheriff's posse of Imperial County. They included an El Centro real estate man, a Brawley fireman, a border Immigration inspector, a general contractor, a paving contractor. They were in a lonely camp, sipping a nip of scotch to brighten the cheer of the fire.

Because of quarantine restrictions, they could not take their horses into Mexico to follow more closely the exact route of the Anza expedition. They had been given permission to ride along the All-American Canal paralleling the border for the next three days. These would be working days in the towns and fields of Imperial County. There would be not even small crowds to recognize what they were doing, assuming that even a small crowd would be permitted to gather along the levee.

We were touched by the unpretentious commitment of   15

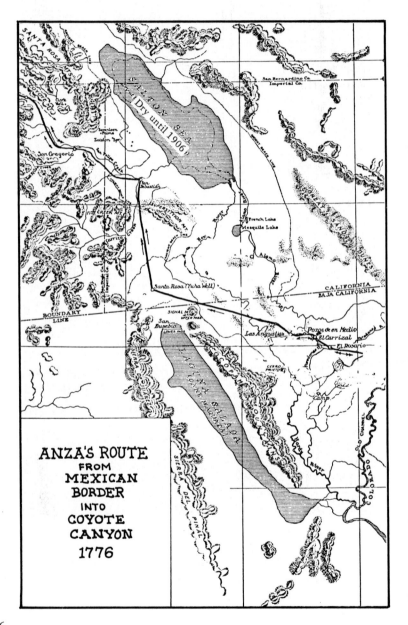

ANZA'S ROUTE
FROM
MEXICAN
BORDER
INTO
COYOTE
CANYON
1776

16

Juan Bautista de Anza, 1736-1788 — explorer, statesman and colonizer. This is his only known portrait, painted in Mexico City in October 1774, little more than a year before he led his expedition across the Colorado River into California.

Anza trail riders around their campfire near Pilot Knob in Imperial County

these few men warming themselves at the Pilot Knob campfire. It gave us a sense of what Helen Shropshire had set in motion up in Monterey two years earlier.

Bicycles and cars can be taken across the border between Calexico and Mexicali without the quarantines that confront horses. You can also walk through customs, if you don't mind a suspicious stare that asks why gringos are walking instead of sitting within the respectable confines of an automobile.

However it may suit your travel style to cross the border, do cross it in order to get an awareness of the changing and unchanged region that was the staging area for the most difficult part of the Anza trail, a desert where death would hover not in a shimmer of heat waves but in the numbing cold of snow and winter winds.

Mexicali is a place of unexpected change for most contemporaty travelers. Father Font would like what's happening in a border city virtually ignored by U.S. travelers since the era when Mexicali Rose was more or less immortalized in song and on film.

During the U.S. prohibition era, it was more wide open with booze and gambling than Tijuana. After gambling was outlawed in the mid-30s, the city changed directions by 180 degrees and settled into quiet agricultural prosperity based on Colorado River irrigation water that changed a Devil's playground.

Today, as capital city of Baja California, with a population base of close to 500,000, Mexicali has unobtrusively become the commercial heart of a rich agricultural empire and a growing center of industry. The federal government and private investors are now setting the next stage—a multimillion dollar program to make Mexicali look like the city it really is.

You won't become aware of what's happening—in this city that should have been named after Juan Bautista de Anza—simply by driving through unimpressive streets on your way to a fishing vacation in San Felipe, or by coming 19

After crossing the Colorado River, Anza didn't challenge the parched desert that was then Imperial County; its searing bleakness had become known in New World mythology as the playground of the Devil. Anza postponed meeting its challenge by turning southward into Baja California, below the present metropolitan area of Mexicali, to follow the trail where he had previously found water. Chief Palma waved them on their way with assurances that Father Garcés and another priest left behind, together with some horses and cattle, would be well cared for until his friend Anza returned.

The promise was kept, but the friendship of the Yumas for travelers from Mexico was not to last much longer. What Father Junipero Serra had warned of in correspondence with the Viceroy-about problems developing along the Mission trail, happened within a few years in the Yuma nation. Soldiers and mule drivers began to take what had been offered to Anze in friendship. The early travelers had been greeted with maidens to warm a cool night. After too many incidents of rape and looting, the Yumas rose up in wrath. Father Garcés, who loved the Indians and had wandered for so long among them, was a tragic victim of the uprising. The Yumas never permitted establishment of a Mission along the Colorado River.

here only to catch a train bound for Guadalajara or Mexico City.

It's necessary to invest a few hours; the investment could produce some unexpected returns, like when I had parked my bicycle and was sitting on the pavement to take a picture of the impressive monument to Benito Juarez.

As I stood up, an attractive young woman stopped her car and asked,

"Are you visiting in our city?"

I told her that I was.

"Thank you," she said.

She smiled sweetly, and drove away.

It's not often in the traveler's world that something like this happens today, especially not in a city that's just as close to the U.S. border as is Tijuana.

The Benito Juarez monument, by the way, could also be a memorial to the Anza expedition. A magnificent piece of sculpture, it shows a young husband and wife and child holding open a copy of Mexico's constitution. We tend to forget within what a brief historical span our own revolution was followed by a revolution that swept Spain out of Mexico.

Not far from the monument, an entire new central city—Centro Civico y Commercial—is being created. In addition to a new Governor's Palace and a vast complex of state and federal agencies, there will be theaters, a Singing Street of restaurants and mariachi bands, a promenade line with handicraft shops, an 11-story deluxe hotel, a new bullring seating 14,000—nearly as large and fully as architecturally creative as the one in Tijuana.

Mexicali's Bellas Artes art center is open now. The university campus, a branch of the University of Mexico, is expanding to include faculties of law and medicine. The city has a new airport, and the old one is being creatively transformed into a recreation center, with an Olympic pool, basketball and tennis courts.

Beyond the city, the most ambitious project is to fill

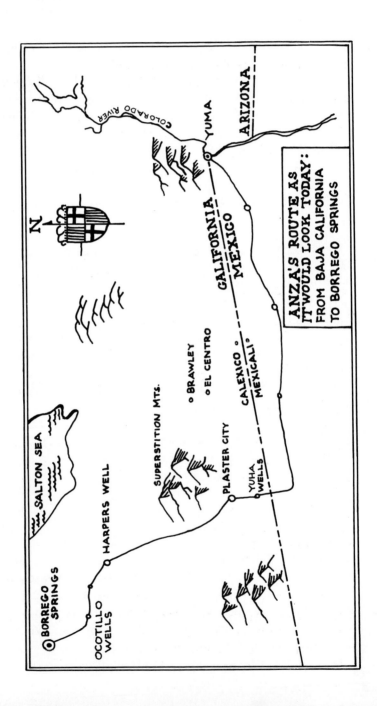

ANZA'S ROUTE AS IT WOULD LOOK TODAY: FROM BAJA CALIFORNIA TO BORREGO SPRINGS

Laguna Salada, near where Anza's expedition made camp, so that yachts can sail in the desert winds.

To see this land as it was in 1775, travel a short distance down and off of Mexico Highway 5, the road to San Felipe. Soon the lush agricultural lands, with small bridges over quiet canals, give way to the timeless desert. The horseman following that dirt trail toward the Sierra de Juarez could be a scout for the Anza expedition.

In Mexicali, as you prepare to trek northward in your personal re-enactment of the expedition, you'll come upon the first of the gracious inns that appear today so unexpectedly along the Anza trail. I should here make the point that in retracing this trail today there are only a relatively few places where any number of people can camp without doing harm to the land; special arrangements in most places had to be made for the horseback riders re-enacting the expedition. And it has long been our personal philosophy that fine inns belong to the walkers, bikers and canoe paddlers of the world, at least as much as to the automobile riders.

We first happened on Lucerna of Mexicali in 1968, the day its candlelit Los Candiles dining room opened. The hotel was designed by Alfonso Amaya, an architect of world stature. Its casitas are built along palm-shaded walks; the pool is fed by a stone aqueduct. The decor of every room was planned around a painting by Carlos Coronado Ortega.

From an overnight bivouac here, it's a short trek to where Anza led his colonists into Imperial County and headed north and west about 8 miles to Yuha Wells. You can locate Yuha Wells on the Southern California Automobile Club map of Imperial County; do get these carefully detailed maps for each county on the way to San Francisco.

We estimate that Anza crossed into California not far from Signal Mountain, which looms like a crouching giant just south of the border. Bicycle westward from here for

By December 6, 1775, the remarkable Father Garcés had recovered enough to overtake the expedition on a solitary journey to visit Indians near the mouth of the Colorado River. But Father Font was troubled by what he self-diagnosed as both ague and flu. He was therefore less than tolerant about the events of the next two days.

First was the fact that Anza, resting his people and livestock for three hard marches ahead, distributed rations of brandy for an evening fandango. "As a result of which," wrote Father Font, "there was great carousing and noise-making among the rabble last night." He forced himself to rouse them for an early Mass, then accosted his Commander: "Sir, it seems that some men were drunk last night." Anza acknowledged there might have been some revelry. Font point out sternly:

"Anyone who gets drunk sins, and anyone who contributes to the drunkenness of others also sins. Only ignorance can absolve him of guilt, and you surely are not ignorant of the intemperance of these people when they drink."

Anza, Font reported, replied with moderation, but showed no repentance. "I note this down," Font wrote, "not through ill will, nor to perpetuate the memory of injuries, but merely in order that it may be inferred from this what caution and patience it is necessary to show with these absolute lords."

Storm clearing — or building?

25

Anza vista point near the Mexican border: "*...how it must have looked in a blizzard to a people who had spent all their lives in warm sunshine...*"

about eight miles until you reach the marker for Anza
Trail Road, a narrow dirt road winding northward into a
desert wilderness that can't have changed appreciably in
200 years. Ride and push your bike two miles up this road
to the now almost forgotten Anza Vista Monument, put
up in 1941 by the De Anza Trail Cabelleros and the Desert
Cavalcade of Imperial County. You'll see the stone
monument silhoutted at the edge of a sheer drop, a quarter
of a mile beyond what appears to be an abandoned
military installation; the structure is still solidly intact and
makes an excellent overnight camp—whether you're
traveling with sleeping bag or camper. The vista to the
north is awesome enough on a sunny day. Think of how it
must have looked in a shrieking blizzard to a people who
had been born in the warm sunshine of Sonora and
Sinaloa. You can drive Anza Trail Road—cautiously.

Return to Highway 98 and bicycle northwestward some
4 miles to the cutoff to Ocotillo, then pedal east again on a
relatively untrafficked byway called Evan Hewes Highway.
Plaster City is principally a U.S. Gypsum plant that won't
tempt you to linger long. Next breather, actually marked
on the county map, is Wind 'n' Sand Cafe. After crossing
the canal to the east, turn north on Huff Road through
cattle country reclaimed from the desert. Signal Mountain
is now a shadow against the horizon behind you, seemingly
as impossible to approach as it was in the grim winter 200
years ago. Reclaimed land gives way to rolling sand dunes
of an eerie beauty. A sign points off into the desolation
towards Superstition Mountain, just to the west of which
the Anza party struggled through driving snow. You feel
with them in this vastness. Huff Road curves past a
restricted wilderness of sand and stone used by the
military for parachute testing. Huff phases into Imler
Road, and this intersects with Forrester.

What we have done here is lead you through the quiet
places of southern Imperial County into the outskirts of
Brawley. It is also as close as you can reasonably come to

Font was as unhappy with the Indians as he was with his Commander. The expedition was now in the territory of the Cajuenches, closely related to the Yumas. He found them gentle, gay and happy—"like simpletons who have never seen anything." The men were robust, the women of good stature and both sexes were to Father Font equally shameless:

"In the matter of incontinence they are so shameless and excessive that I do not believe that in all the world there is another tribe that is worse. The women, it might be said, are common, and the hospitality which they show their guests is to provide them with companions. . . . ."

Font said Mass with vigor. Anza divided his expedition into three sections to cope with the scarcity of water and the increasingly bitter weather that loomed ahead. Yuha Wells, known to him as Santa Rosa of the Flat Rocks, would be dried up for a week if the entire party arrived at one time. They passed close to Signal Mountain, which Father Garcés earlier had named Cerro del Impossible. The cold grew more severe. Father Garcés waved goodby and went on his lonely way. Font wrote:

"Father Garcés is so well fitted to get along with the Indians that he appears to be but an Indian himself. He sits with them in a circle at night around the fire, with his legs crossed . . . talking with them with much serenity and deliberation. And although the foods of the Indians are as nasty and dirty as those outlandish peoples themselves, the father eats with great gusto . . . In short, God has created him, as I see it, solely for the purpose of seeking out these unhappy, ignorant and rustic people."

Anza's route. The area through which he must have passed is now broken with great sections of military reserve. To the east is the parachute testing area around Superstition Mountain. On the west is the Carrizo Impact Area, closed to the public. Up the center, partially intersecting the route of the U.S. Gypsum narrow gauge railroad, is another section marked for live bombing. If all the impacting could be confined to one area, it would be simple enough to mark Anza's route of history with a desert trail comparable to the way to the Vista monument. The desert on either side of the trail could be declared off-limits, as in a state or national park.

Should you be driving the trail we have marked, you can continue up Forrester into the town of Westmoreland and then on to a more than gracious overnight at Casa del Zorro in Anza-Borrego State Park. But a biker has already come far enough for one day—approximately 50 miles from the border crossing point. Don't be dismayed at the prospect of a night in Brawley. Continue up rural Carter Road, along the canal, to a choice of comfortable accommodations in Brawley. The Packin' Shed, built of natural wood and hung with cargo netting, is another of those intriguing and little known restaurants you'll be coming upon during the next several hundred miles.

From Brawley, bike back to Forrester Road to avoid Highway 86 traffic on the way to Westmoreland. Again you are in farming and ranching country, although Cesar Chavez and his farm workers might not always find things as tranquil here as they appear to the passerby.

After Westmoreland, ride with alertness along Highway 86 for some 16 miles to the turnoff into Highway 78, a wide two-lane road with marked shoulders that make for safe bicycling. Except for dune buggies and dune cycles tearing up the desert around Ocotillo Wells on a bright weekend, the vista is calming—misted by the Salton Sea, which didn't exist when Anza passed this way; the Colorado River didn't overflood into the Salton basin until   29

At Yuha Wells, Anza watered his livestock before dawn so that the wells would have a chance to refill before the next section of the expedition arrived. He got up at two o'clock in the morning to do the same at the camp near Plaster City. His first division —Father Font riding in his assigned position directly behind the tail of Anza's horse—made about twelve miles in the next four hours, and then halted where they found firewood and pasturage. Anza wrote tersely that the storm "was threatening from all directions."

They waited at Harper's Well for the other two divisions. Their own cattle, horses and mules began to freeze to death during the night. Yet the people benefited from the rest. Anza noted: "Whereas nine days ago we counted more than fifteen invalids, three of them dangerously ill, today there are less than five of the first class and none of the second." He attributed part of the recovery to the many watermelons given them a few days earlier by the Indians.

In their joy at being reunited, these incredible people threw a fandango in the teeth of the gathering storm. The merry widow enlivened things by singing bawdy songs. Father Font was outraged, though he conceded her songs were "applauded and cheered." Finally the man with whom she had reached an amiable arrangement for the trip got jealous and wanted to beat her. Font was all for the beating, and objected when Anza came out of his tent to prevent it. The fandango continued on through the wild, freezing desert night. Father Font raised hell about it at Mass the next morning.

early in our own century. Watch for Los Puertecitos monument along the roadside. A plaque will tell you that "Juan Bautista de Anza's expedition passed through this little pass on December 19, 1775," enroute from Harper's Well and Ocotillo Wells to Borrego.

Turn off Highway 78 into Borrego Springs Road—Casa del Zorro is close to its intersection with Yaqui Pass Road. Another 50-mile-day of not severe bicycling.

Father Font's sermon compared the fandango to "festivities in honor of the devil," and he wondered why Anza had been more concerned about the chastisement of the widow than about the "scandal" of the party itself. "I do not think the Commander liked this very well," he wrote in his diary. "He did not speak to me once during the whole morning. I suppose he was offended. . . ."

Anza may have had more on his mind. The expedition traveled about twelve miles in four hours to a watering place he called San Gregorio. You'll find it on your county map as Borrego Sink. The desolation of the Borrego Badlands was directly to the northeast. His route would be to the northwest, up Coyote Canyon to the cresting of the Sierras—which loomed before these people of Sonora and Sinaloa as a dreadful barrier of snow and ice.

The waterhole at San Gregorio was exhausted before all of the saddle animals were watered, and the cattle had not yet arrived. Anza directed the digging of more wells. The water flowed slowly. When the cattle arrived at night, four had died during the short march. Anza wrote in his diary: "This night was so extremely cold that three saddle animals and five head of cattle were frozen to death, and the weather was so hard on our people that almost none of them slept, for they spent the night occupied in feeding the fires in order to withstand it. . . ." Father Font suffered from flu and shook with frequent chills. Of the morning, he confessed: "I wished to say Mass, but I could not do so on account of the intense cold." This was five days before Christmas—December 20, 1775.

IV.
Coyote Canyon to Anza

The wonder of the Anza trail today is that the route up Coyote Canyon through Anza-Borrego State Park is still only a jeep trail. Developers in Borrego Springs came close to getting a highway in 1973, but the dedicated State Park rangers—aided by people who had bought luxury homes from these same developers—blocked the move.

You won't be able to travel this part of the Anza trail unless you have a jeep, a horse or can carry your own backpack. San Diego County riders for the Re-enactment Committee rode their horses up Coyote Canyon. Our plan was to backpack the Canyon after bicycling to the end of Di Giorgio Road in Borrego Springs. You can approximate the terrain by driving Highway S22 to Warner Springs, then continuing on to the town of Anza through Aguanga.

We arrived in Borrego Springs the day after Thanksgiving, and about two weeks ahead of the Re-enactment Committee riders. The weather staged its own re-enactment. A blizzard turned the mountains to snow and ice. Cold rain slanted across the valley. Since we were charting this route for others who would travel it during the Bicentennial and subsequent years, we didn't try to recreate 1775 by camping out in Borrego Sink. We gratefully checked into the comforts of Casa del Zorro to

Leaving Borrego Sink at 9 o'clock on the morning of December 20, Anza led his expedition for about twelve miles across the floor of the valley to a crossing of Coyote Creek close to where our own hike would begin. He called the campsite El Vado, The Ford. It later came to be known as Beatty's Ranch. Anza wrote: "At seven o'clock at night the cattle which had set out ahead of us from San Gregorio arrived at the camp, eleven of them having died because they were completely worn out. . ."

Five Indians fled from El Vado at the sight of the approaching expedition, leaving behind vessels in which they were gathering seeds. With the intuitive understanding that was to mark his entire career on the frontier, Anza noted in his diary: "I gave orders that they not be pursued, lest they might consider it an act of violence. Their vessels, a bow and three of their blankets of jackrabbit skin which they left behind, I caused to be gathered up and placed where they could find them. . . ." Father Font also wrote of this incident, and added: "They are a people with degenerate bodies, and are very miserable and timid."

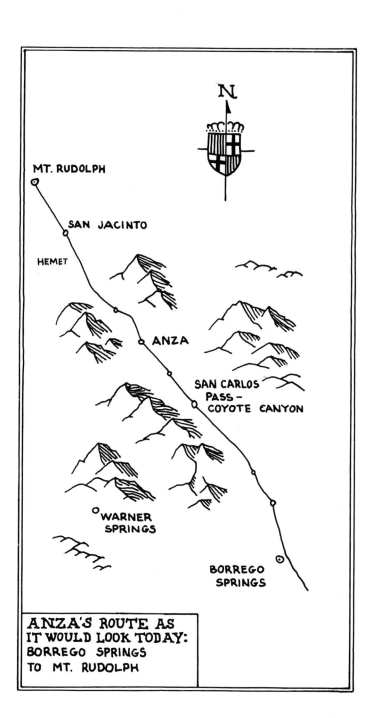

N

MT. RUDOLPH

SAN JACINTO

HEMET

ANZA

SAN CARLOS
PASS –
COYOTE CANYON

WARNER
SPRINGS

BORREGO
SPRINGS

ANZA'S ROUTE AS
IT WOULD LOOK TODAY:
BORREGO SPRINGS
TO MT. RUDOLPH

"....it seemed prudent to carry bivouac supplies and a sleeping bag rated to twenty degrees below...(Photo of Frank Riley at entrance to Coyote Canyon)

wait out the storm. In early afternoon, the weather cleared for a couple of hours—enough time for us to get acquainted with the trail by hiking to the first creek crossing. We got back before the storm closed the canyon again. The wind had a piercing chill, a sound of wild and lonely places. Snow falling in the mountains and rain in the valley created a rainbow that was sheer fantasy. Two hundred years ago suddenly came into perspective as an incredibly short span in the history of the desert and snow crests around us.

The storm that forced us to linger in Borrego Springs gave us a chance to learn something of this history, and of the circumstances that made it possible to preserve the most dramatic part of the Anza trail within a state park.

The state part concept—for the nation as well as California—began in 1864, when President Abraham Lincoln authorized a federal grant transferring the area known as Yosemite Valley and the Mariposa Grove of Redwoods to California. These areas were later to be returned to the federal government, but out of the basic concept have come more than 200 state park units in California alone—among them the half-million acres of Anza-Borrego, the nation's largest state park. Most of the lower-level acres were a prehistoric ocean, and later an ancient lake. Animal fossils date back more than a million years. Along walking trails you come upon grinding rocks used by Indians a thousand years ago. Anza was not the first non-Indian to travel through Coyote Canyon. In 1772, Lieutenant Pedro Fages of the San Diego Presidio descended the canyon from the Pacific Coast in pursuit of deserters. When Butterfield Overland Mail coaches from St. Louis traveled the southern route toward Pueblo de Los Angeles in the 1850s, they chose mountain passes well to the south of Coyote Canyon; otherwise, this remarkably preserved section of the Anza trail might well be a four-lane highway today.

37

Anza kept his people at El Vado until December 23, waiting for a sergeant to arrive with other cattle left behind to rest. Fifty of them died before reaching the ford. Anza recorded on December 22: "All this day it has been threatening to rain, and it actually began at eleven o'clock at night . . . we thought that in the sierra nearest to us it was snow which was falling. . . ."

All that day, Father Font was troubled with his flu, which was getting, as he wrote, much worse. Indians, realizing that Anza wanted to be a friend, began returning to the ford. Anza fed them. Father Font could see little promise among them of future converts to Christ. "In fine," he wrote, "they are so savage, wild and dirty, disheveled, ugly, small and timid, that only because they have the human form is it possible to believe that they belong to mankind."

But when his own pains eased, Father Font could become the scholarly theologian: "Shall we think that God created these men merely to condemn them to the Inferno, after passing in this world a life so miserable? By no means! . . . Shall we say that God condemns them without guilt? This cannot be, because it would be contrary to His justice, and it is certain that *Perditio tua ex te* . . . And I piously believe that those beasts whom God will save are those ignorant Indians and helpless heathen, who are without doubt the beasts of human kind. . . ."

Of the delay at El Vado, Font commented: "Perhaps these delays and losses irritated the commander. At any rate, today he stayed in his tent and I in mine, without talking together or seeing each other except at the dinner hours. . . ."

For your own retracing of the Anza route during the coming year or years, plan to spend at least as much time in this State Park as Anza did. From late autumn through spring are the kindliest months; you won't often be greeted by a snow storm. We've been here in the early spring, when the desert was a carpet of wild flowers. Along more than 700 miles of trails, you'll come upon oases of fan palms, wild plum and apricot, elephant trees, tamarisks, live oak and cottonwood. Creekbeds are lush with vegetation; badlands totally barren. Sandstone canyons have been sculptured into galleries of surrealism by a million years of wind and rain. The night is filled with stars, and the air is sweet to breathe.

The entire wilderness is patrolled by only ten rangers, under Chief Ranger Bud Getty; some rangers have a beat that covers 100,000 acres. They somehow find time to lead nature walks, and to talk about their park during evenings around a campfire. Part of their time is spent in protecting urban visitors from dangers inherent in all desert and mountain travel, but far more time is devoted to protecting the fragility of nature from human thoughtlessness. It can take up to fifteen generations for nature to recover from damages around a careless campsite. Each visitor receives a leaflet headed: "You are responsible—you are the answer to Anza-Borrego's survival as a first-rate desert park."

For those who don't come to camp, Borrego Springs could be one of the State Park's major surprises. With splendid hotels, restaurants, golf courses and tennis courts, it has become an attractive resort in its own right, reflecting diverse cultures. The Mall Restaurant is maintained by Inge and Wolfgang Schumann, who came to Borrego from Switzerland via Hawaii. It's agreeably startling in this desert town to pick up a wine menu offering Beameister Liebfraumilch and Cruse Chateauneuf du Pape. La Casa del Zorro began life as a simple adobe ranch house in 1937. It grew slowly into the lodge called

At daylight on Saturday, December 23, it was raining, but the rain stopped at nine o'clock and Anza gave the order to march up the canyon. The rain started again before they could mount. It was a cold rain driven by a bitter wind, and the trail was ascending now. The colonists could cover only four miles before being forced to camp at Santa Catharina Springs in the Lower Willows. With darkness, the storm became more severe. Indians appeared, bringing a little firewood and a present of food for Anza. Father Font, shaking with chills in the driving rain, wrote of the bringing of gifts but concluded with the judgement that these Indians were basically "malevolent, bad-hearted, and evil-intentioned, although very cowardly."

Despite continuing rain on the day of Christmas Eve, Anza took his people on up the canyon for nine miles to the next camp at Fig Tree Springs. Fog and mists were so thick it was impossible to see the hills around the canyon. To his horror, Father Font learned that Anza was about to distribute a Christmas Eve ration of brandy. At dinner, he accosted his commander:

"Sir, although my opinion is of no value and I do not cut any figure here, I can do no less than to tell you that I have learned that there is drinking today."

"Yes, there is," Anza replied quietly.

"Well, Sir," Font said severely, "I wish to say that it does not seem to me right that we should celebrate the birth of the Infant Jesus with drunkenness."

Anza replied, as previously, that he did not distribute a ration of brandy for the purpose of getting people drunk. Font retorted, as he had in Mexico, that one who cooperates with those who might drink to excess also sins. He then retired to his tent, to listen with outrage to the singing and dancing of another "very noisy" fandango. "Such," he wrote in resignation, "is the rule of these absolute lords."

The Desert Resort. In 1960, James A. Copley made it a part of his newspaper empire, and undertook the expansion and improvements that resulted in today's Casa. The cuisine does have an international reputation. Guest bungalows have sitting rooms as well as kingsize beds and private patios. Firelight in the lodge flickers on brass, copperwork and pewter. Original oil paintings and water colors from the Copley collection tell the story of the west beginning with early Indian life.

Hopefully, we set our alarm for 5 A.M. A cold wind drove the rain against our patio window. When the alarm went off, there was still a dripping from the eaves, but we looked out to the glory of a sky filled with stars.

Because of the way the weather had been changing almost on the hour, I didn't want to take Elfriede up the canyon. We phoned the Highway Patrol in San Diego and were told the mountain roads were closed by snow and ice, but this obviously was a recording made the previous evening. Elfriede would check again later in the morning, and would try to drive with our bicycles to meet me near Anza, where Coyote Canyon came up into the Sierra high country. I wore a down parka and winter hiking clothes; it also seemed prudent to carry bivouac supplies and a sleeping bag rated to twenty degrees below zero.

The sun rose as I started up Coyote Canyon, and was never shadowed by a cloud all day. My regret at every step was that Elfriede couldn't be along to share what has to be one of the rarest hiking trails in all of California. I didn't reckon with her ingenuity.

From Chief Ranger Bud Getty we had learned there was a climb of some fourteen miles to a stone monument marking the Anza campsite where a child was born on Christmas eve, 1775. It was four miles more to Turkey Track, formed by the intersection of three canyons. A steeper ascent up Turkey Track would lead to the end of a dirt road cutting across the mesa from the town of Anza.

The life-giving artery of Coyote Canyon is a creek that

During the fandango, the wife of a soldier began to experience pains of impending childbirth. Father Font put aside his own sickness and outrage and went to her tent to "console and encourage her as best I could." A half hour before midnight, he reported, "she very happily and quickly gave birth to a boy."

On a raw and overcast Christmas morning, Font rose to the challenge of both the fandango and the Christmas Eve birth. He said no less than three Masses, and insisted that all be fully attended, in order that the colonists could show appropriate repentance and thanksgiving. As usual on such special occasions, he committed his sermon to his diary. It leaned heavily on Latin phraseology attributed to St. John and St. Paul. Font made their learned admonitions specific by addressing himself to Christmas Eve "eating and drinking, and fandangos and drunkenness, and noise and lewdness." And his noble voice rolled out across Coyote Canyon: "Oh, earth, earth, how you change everything!"

At the end of the third Mass, he solemnly baptized the boy Salvador Ignacio, son of Ignacio and Gertrudis Rivas Linares.

Salvador Ignacio and his parents went on to become one of the founding families of San Francisco. He may or may not have been the first immigrant child born in California—some women from Mexico had already made their way up Baja California to join husbands at the presidio of San Diego—but if his parents had come from Boston instead of Sinaloa, and had he been christened Henry or Patrick, his name would have been known to every child who ever studied California history.

flows all year from the seepage of springs, and sometimes floods from heavy rains and the runoff of melting snows. This morning it was full enough with rain to ripple over polished rocks. Working my way up the canyon meant continually crossing and re-crossing it. Willows and tamarisks closed overhead in the narrow reaches, and then there would be a widening into broad, alluvial plains, closing again into smaller canyons topped by snow peaks edged sharp against the blue sky.

Every life form of the Anza-Borrego can be found somewhere in Coyote Canyon. Kit fox, grey fox, coyotes, bobcats, mountain lions and mule deer depend on the creek for drinking water, but the hiker seldom sees them. Even more difficult to glimpse is the Borrego Bighorn venturing down from the heights. More than 150 varieties of birds—mockingbirds, quail, dove and the swift roadrunner, swift enough to run down and kill a rattlesnake— are at home in the long canyon. It was in one of the narrows that I shared a trail with the unafraid humming-bird.

Anza colonists battled the weather for five days to cover the route I was hiking in winter sunshine. I found one ocotillo still in flower. Coyote Canyon near Santa Catarina Springs was a quiet broken only by the wind in the willows. In Collins Valley, just beyond Santa Catarina, an inquisitive jackrabbit kept hopping across my trail. On Christmas morning of 1851, precisely three-quarters of a century after the Anza party had passed through here, peaceful Collins Valley was the scene of an Indian uprising, and the killing of five of their chiefs by San Diego Volunteers under Major Heintzelman. The boundary of Los Coyotes Indian Reservation is now a half dozen miles to the southwest of Collins Valley. Coyotes Indians declined to take part in any Bicentennial proceedings. Tribal councils of the Yumas and Apaches also voted not to participate, stating there was nothing in the Bicentennial for them to celebrate.

43

". . . . near Middle Willows in Coyote Canyon was a cool, green silence. . . ."

Sheep Canyon Natural Preserve is between Collins Valley and the Los Coyotes Reservation. Palms grow out of the rocks in Sheep Valley. Bighorns feel secure in crevasses of the high, jagged cliffs. Having this area declared a Natural Preserve was one maneuver used to block the building of a four-lane highway up Coyote Canyon.

From Collins Valley, my personal re-enactment trek led into Yucca Valley, a vista that showed how much I'd been climbing—as well as what was still ahead. I sat on a rock in the bright sun for a lunch that might have caused Father Font to lift an eyebrow: Granola mixed with nuts, coconut and wheat germ; and See's Candy peanut brittle for dessert.

After the Salvador Canyon turnoff, Middle Willows was cool, green silence. The willows formed a canopy over the gurgling creek. Then there were more rocks than willows, and the wind whistling down from Sierra snows was so strong against my backpack that I thought of repacking in order to put the sleeping bag beneath instead of on top of the pack frame.

My two trail maps indicated I was probably within a half mile of where the Christmas Eve baby was born at Fig Tree Spring, just below San Carlos Pass. A sound behind me was too strong to be the wind in the rocky gorge. After all our travels around the world, I should have known what to expect before I looked back to see Elfriede bouncing over the boulders in a jeep piloted by Park Ranger John Ruddley—who had been beguiled to take her along on his daily trail check so that she could see how I was doing. They confirmed that the monument to the child's birth was not far ahead. I caught up with them there in about ten minutes.

The monument, formed of stones washed down from the mountains, stands close to the trail. A plaque telling of the birth of Salvador Ignacio was placed there on May 7, 1950, by the California Centennials Commission; the stone 45

Lonely monument in Coyote Canyon to the first immigrant child born in California.

46

Elfriede Riley and Ranger John Rudley at Child Monument in Coyote Canyon.

Survival shelter in Coyote Canyon: ". . .I would like to have Governor Jerry Brown walk up Coyote Canyon with me to dedicate this lonely survival hut to Senora Gertrudis Lenares, California's first madonna. . ."

48

base was built by a then active association called Roads to Romance.

Chief Ranger Bud Getty had told us the day before that the wives of two of his rangers were in their last month of pregnancy, and had offered to cooperate with the De Anza Bicentennial re-enactment by having their babies born in the survival hut near the child monument. They could find no enthusiasm for the project, not even from their own husbands.

Elfriede and Ranger John Ruddley went on up a side canyon to make sure all was well with two backpackers he had dropped off there just before the Thanksgiving Day storm. I continued up Coyote Canyon and soon came to the survival shelter. It was made of stone and appeared to be an old sheep or cattle herder's hut. A log was braced against the door to hold it shut against winds that could sweep so strongly down the canyon. A hand-lettered sign up on the door advised: "Please take your own trash and try not to shoot up or dirty up this cabin—it might have to shelter you from a cold storm."

There's a well behind the hut. With some refurbishment, this place of survival could be brought up to the standard of similar shelters we've seen in the Swiss Alps and in the Snowy Mountains of Australia. We would like to provide for this refurbishment, and have the state name the shelter after Senora Gertrudis Lenares, California's first madonna. Another hope, a rather wistful one, is to have Governor Jerry Brown walk up Coyote Canyon with me to dedicate this lonely survival hut. It would say something about the Bicentennial to the Mexican-American people of California.

Anza wrote of the morning after Christmas: "The mother was better and had the pluck to march." The morning began brightly, but rain started at nine o'clock again. It turned to sleet as the route ascended the steepest part of the canyon. At the end of the day, Anza noted mater-of-factly: "With this march, the sierra or cordillera which runs to and ends at Baja California is now overcome. . . ."

Anza, in his diary for December 27, described the high mesa around the area of the town to be named after him as "level country with an abundance of the best pasturage, trees and grass that we have seen thus far."

He also noted: "All the sierras which we have seen today in the direction of the South Sea are so snow-covered that scarcely any trees can be seen on the summits." It is this aspect, not the rolling pasturelands, that impressed and depressed the people of his expedition. It seemed to them that they had survived Coyote Canyon only to reach cold country that would grow progressively colder as they moved northward.

"As a result," Anza wrote, "they have become so melancholy that some of the women had to weep. Through their tears they managed to say, 'If so many animals died of cold and the people nearly died in places where there was less snow, how will it be in the place where we see so much of it?' " He added: "I checked these complaints by various counsels, telling them that the cold would be moderated when we got to the coast and its missions. . . ."

Camp was made this night at the beginning of Bautista Canyon, near Tripp Flat.

V.

Anza to Mission Inn

· If you've driven up S22 from Borrego Springs instead of hiking Coyote Canyon, there's still a way for you to see something of the Canyon—and even to get to the Child Monument without too much of a walk.

Drive on from Warner Springs to Aguanga, and then up Cahuilla Road (Highways 73-373) into Anza. The county map will guide you a couple of miles more into Terwilliger Road. Two miles south of Terwilliger, a dirt road takes off eastward across the fields. It is marked with a signpost: Coyote Canyon Road. In good weather, especially with a car like our VW, you can follow it almost to the Turkey Track descent. A four-wheel drive, of course, will take you all the way. From Turkey Track, it's a pleasant walk of no more than an hour to the survival hut and monument.

Bicyclists take over the Anza trail again at the inter-section of Coyote Canyon Road and Terwilliger. This is high rolling mountain mesa known to relatively few coastal Californians, and almost never seen by out-of-state visitors. The air blows free across a great expanse of valley. Working and weekend ranchers live like the Dons of old on spreads with such names as Rolling Hills of Anza. Anza's main street is along the highway through town. People here are trusting of their neighbors in a way that doesn't happen too often anymore; we saw the lady in the grocery

Father Font was still plagued with aches and chills, and consequently short of temper. He exploded with outrage when Anza sent a messenger to his tent asking if he had any mail to send ahead by courier to Mission San Gabriel. "Why must I write now, when it is so late?" he demanded. "The commander must have decided to do this several days ago—and now he lets me know about it at the last minute! Well, tell him that I will write when we reach camp tomorrow if there is time, and if not I'll have patience." After duly recording this in his diary, Font added his customary comment: "I note these things down in order that they may serve as light by which it may be seen that in such journeys and with such lords it is necessary to arm oneself with patience."

Anza kept the expedition an additional day at the Bautista Canyon camp. Senora Gertrudis Linares was suffering with severe pains, perhaps because of resuming the jolting march so soon after childbirth. She recovered enough by the next morning for the expedition to proceed down the canyon.

Both Anza and Font recorded in their diaries that they were welcomed into Southern California by an earthquake of about four minutes duration.

The descent into San Jacinto Valley did wonders for Father Font's health and disposition. Anza seemed less like an absolute lord. Font wrote that "I was greatly relieved of my ills," and that "today I was on rather good terms with the commander, and we talked a little on the way. . . ."

store cash a $100 check for a man rather than send him on down the road to the bank. At the service station not far from the Anza Community Church, the owner-attendant had time to talk. "Anza's changing," he said. "Folks from down below are discovering what we have up here, and they want a piece of it." He waved his arm down the highway-main street. "Why, nine years ago, you wouldn't have seen anybody along here. . . . ." But he still wouldn't live anywhere else on earth. Signs on the roads into Anza list a Bicentennial year population of 700.

There are memorable trails from Anza to Hemet for both walkers and bikers. Afoot—and in fair weather by car—you can most closely follow the original Anza route.

Bautista Canyon Road is a good dirt road today; Riverside County has been grading it more often of late. Winter storms occasionally close it down, but at other times you can drive its 16-mile length to Valle Vista and Hemet in a family car. We found it an easy and scenic downhill walk.

We also tried a route for cyclists by following mountain Highway 74 past Lake Hemet and through Mountain Center, the turnoff to Idyllwild. Except for a two-mile ascent from Lake Hemet Store to Keene Summit, these 31 miles of paved road are first level, then a long downhill braking coast. Do hang tight to the edge on the curves, for the two-lane road is rather narrow. Much of the early section, though, is safe biking through the well-tended San Bernardino National Forest.

A vista turnout point just above the 4000-foot elevation marker on Highway 74 gives you a quiet moment to share the feelings of the Anza families as they looked for the first time from the cold and snow down into the valley of hope, the kind of California that had been promised to them.

The next thousand feet of descent follows a deep canyon. In another five miles, you are out of the San Bernardino forest and into the flatlands of Valle Vista.

San Jacinto Valley was then known as the Valley of St. Joseph, and it contained a lake which has since vanished. Font wrote of "a valley so leafy that because of its beauty and attractiveness we called it Paradise Valley." He grew poetic about the crystalline and beautiful water, and the softness of the land. He felt that both the San Jacinto River Camp and the next near Mt. Rudolph would make splendid sites for settlements, and that the Indians presented reasonably human possibilities for conversion to Christ.

On the day of New Year's eve, approaching the vicinity of what would someday be the city of Riverside, Father Font became even more poetical about rosemary and sunflowers in bloom, and "grapevines and wild grapes of such good stock that it looked like a vineyard."

Anza was concerned about the loss of a bull and a horse in fording the then deep and swift Santa Ana River. Font noted this loss, along with his observations about the crystalline beauty of the water.

And his diary of that New Year's eve contains no mention of a brandy ration, a fandango or a merry widow's songs.

Highway 74 leads on into Hemet's Florida Avenue, which may change your preconceptions about this town. The avenue is bright, alive—with temptations like Sir George's Smorgasbord House, The Embers, the Railroader Restaurant and the Blue Vest. Arrows will intrigue you toward Ramona Bowl and Mt. San Jacinto College, Seven Hills and Echo Hills Country Clubs.

During our research on the Anza trail, we came across an echo of concerns from another era in the April 2, 1951 issue of Southern California's long-defunct *Fortnight* Magazine. The article told of an effort by Hemet and Borrego Springs to convince the State Highway Commission that a road ought to be built over the Anza trail up Coyote Canyon. The argument was that such a road would cut off fifty miles of travel between Imperial Valley and Los Angeles, and in the dawning era of the California freeway boom such an argument could have been persuasive.

The idea first occured to Mrs. Ruth E. Peters, who became secretary-manager of the Hemet Chamber of Commerce in 1947. With her husband Karl, she organized the first cavalcade of jeeps between Hemet and Borrego with the hope of dramatizing the need for a road over the Anza trail. Incredibly, this annual pilgrimage has persisted more than a quarter of a century. Another ride is scheduled for the Bicentennial year of 1976, although the last major thrust for such a road was blocked three years ago, when Anza-Borrego Park rangers and Borrego townspeople joined to defeat the well-financed move by Borrego developers. Karl Peters is dead, his widow lives in retirement in Hemet, and Carl Newbower, manager of the Hemet Chamber of Commerce, wonders how much longer the cavalcade itself can be continued. It now has to cross private lands as well as State Park preserves. "We didn't want a super highway in the first place," Newbower recalls. "We really just wanted a small road. . . ."

Bicycle San Jacinto Street for two miles out of Hemet

Looking back down the main street of Anza: "...a high rolling mountain mesa known to relatively few coastal Californians..."

to the town of San Jacinto, about three miles from Anza's camp on the San Jacinto River. Ramona Boulevard and then Ramona Expressway out of San Jacinto pass just to the north of his next camp near Mt. Rudolph. We found the Ramona "Expressway" to be a misnomer. It is a delight of a road for bypassing the freeways into Riverside—a surprise for cyclists, with wide marked shoulders. It angles around the Lake Perris State Recreation area.

About ten miles from its beginning at Ramona Boulevard-Highway 79, Ramona Expressway crosses Perris Boulevard. Turn north here to Alessandro Boulevard and follow it into Riverside the backcountry way. Before reaching Anza's next camp—a few miles west of Mt. Rubidoux, you may want to bivouac at the old Mission Inn in Riverside.

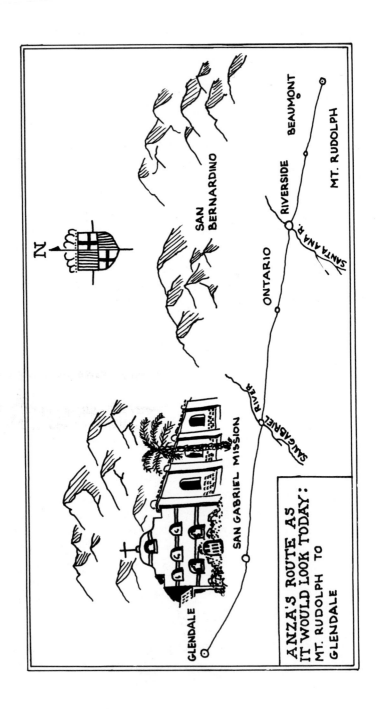

N

SAN BERNARDINO

BEAUMONT

MT. RUDOLPH

RIVERSIDE

ONTARIO

SANTA ANA R.

SAN GABRIEL RIVER

SAN GABRIEL MISSION

GLENDALE

ANZA'S ROUTE AS
IT WOULD LOOK TODAY:
MT. RUDOLPH TO
GLENDALE

VI.
Mission Inn to San Gabriel

From the beginning, almost two years ago, when we first thought of retracing the De Anza Trail in as tranquil a way as possible this late in the 20th century, the sections of it between Riverside and the west San Fernando Valley seemed to pose the greatest challenge. It wouldn't be the physical challenge of Coyote Canyon, or the harassment we expected to encounter in trying to round Point Conception by land; rather, it would be the apparent impossibility of approximating anything like the Anza passage through what had become the megalopolis of Greater Los Angeles, a spread of suburbia and essentially satellite cities laced together by freeways and streets dedicated to maximum motor traffic. The idea of a peaceful bicycle trail through all of this seemed pure fantasy, and more than mildly suicidal.

When we finally worked it out, the route surprised us as much as it may surprise you. If you can't bike or walk at least parts of it, take the time to drive it slowly. You'll see what we've all been missing these swiftly passing freeway years.

Riverside's Mission Inn will condition your psyche for the experience. In 1876, the first centennial after the Anza pioneers camped near Mt. Rubidoux, Frank Miller came west with his engineer father and family. The following year, to add a survival base to an engineer's economic life, 59

On New Year's morning, Father Font remained in a mellow mood. His diary began simply: "Monday, January 1, 1776: I said Mass, and in it I said a few words to the people concerning the character of the holiday, exhorting them to renew their good resolutions, since we were now beginning a new year, etc."

The couriers Anza had sent ahead to Mission San Gabriel returned with a gift of seventeen horses sent by the padres to relieve the expedition's weary, bone-thin mounts. The couriers also brought a message that would soon lead to a decision to encamp the families in the expedition for almost two months at San Gabriel. There had been an Indian uprising at the San Diego Mission. A padre and two servants had been killed; all of the few soldiers of the guard had been wounded. The father ministers at San Gabriel were apprehensive that the uprising might·spread to their own mission.

Anza had already made a reluctant decision to follow the mission route to Monterey. As a matter of personal pride, he would have preferred to blaze a new trail through Cajon Pass above Riverside and on up the eastern Sierra before crossing over to the coast; it galled him a bit to have to follow in the path of Portolá and Father Serra. But he knew that his people and livestock could not survive more winter cold. He sent word to Monterey so that missions along the route could be supplied to receive his expedition.

the family built a few cottages close to the Riverside stagecoach stop. Passengers found them pleasant for overnight stays. From this base, Frank Miller eventually built his Mission Inn, which has been described by many adjectives—including bizarre. There's no doubt Miller had the rococo eye of a William Randolph Hearst—whose *other* castle we were to encounter so unexpectedly further north along the Anza trail. Frank Miller also had the Hearstian vision, along with a sense of discipline that often eluded William Randolph. There would never be, for example, a Byzantine gilt dome on Mission Inn. Miller did assemble artifacts from around the world, yet he housed them in a way that cradled the revival of California Mission architecture. And he created one of the few grand hotels in America to be designated as an official state and national historical landmark.

Presidents McKinley, Taft and Teddy Roosevelt were guests at Mission Inn. So was King Gustav of Sweden. An ambitious young lawyer named Richard Milhaus Nixon and his schoolteacher sweetheart were married at the Inn, although a plaque may not memorialize this event until well into another centennial century. With Frank Miller's passing, his Inn slowly slipped off the stagecoach route of history. Today, it is just as slowly being restored to its one-time grandeur. About a dozen of the original 65 rooms have again become period pieces. Boutiques and galleries are starting to line the old Arcade. The Music Room with its 2,000-pipe organ, the Court of the Orient, the St. Francis Atrio, the Bacchus Fountain, the dragon tree of the Mandarin's Journey, the Lealea Room, Writer's Row and the International Rotunda can again be visited in the odyssey of a guided tour. The comeback has to inch along, as income and the economy permit. An excellent kitchen serving the Spanish Patio Restaurant helps with the income. If the income can be sustained, a grand hotel will be saved.

Try to save this next portion of the Anza trail for a

Leaving Mt. Rubidoux on a day that turned to heavy rain, the expedition crossed the Jurupa hills near Pedley, and camped on San Antonio Creek, not far from the future city of Ontario. The final camp was made on San Gabriel Wash, east of the present site of the Mission, to where it had been moved since Anza had been through here in 1774.

The expedition reached Mission San Gabriel shortly before noon on January 4, 1776—seventy-four days after leaving Tubac and eight months after setting out from the homeland in Mexico. Anza had brought his people through the long journey with a net gain of two: Three children had been born to offset the death of the mother in childbirth. Father Font wrote of their reception at San Gabriel:

"Captain Commander of Monterey, Don Fernando Rivera y Moncada, who was on his way to San Diego because of the uprising there, and the father minister of San Gabriel, Fray Antonio Paterna, came out on the road to welcome us. Our coming was a matter of great rejoicing by everybody. The guard of the mission welcomed us with a volley, and the two other fathers who were there, Father Fray Antonio Cruzado and Father Fray Miguel Sanchez, had us greeted with many peals of bells, and with special demonstrations of joy."

Sunday. Bicycle north on University Avenue, then follow Mission Boulevard out of Riverside. Just before the bridge over the Santa Ana wash, the mood of the route will be established by a picnic retreat around a stone grotto down which water trickles. Riverview and Limonite Avenues lead around Mt. Rubidoux and westward south of Mira Loma.

You are on a biking road through a rural landscape. Limonite isn't a road you'll find on any map but a county map of Riverside County. Sam's Feed and Western Wear emporium is immediately west of Pedley Road intersection. Limonite phases into Cloverdale Road and dairy-land. Massive old eucalyptus trees shade gracious ranch homes. Dairies proudly display their Awards of Merit signs. Follow Archibald, then Pine. Grain fields reach across a broad valley. A cheese-making plant at Euclid may remind you, as it did us, of Wisconsin dairy country. Hay sheds add to the illusion, as do cows feeding through iron grillwork in front of their troughs. Central Avenue will turn you northward past poultry ranches. Remind yourself that you *are* on the way from Riverside to Los Angeles.

Cross under Freeway 60 and wonder where everyone is going so fast. Entering Montclair, turn west on Holt Avenue, which melds into Valley Boulevard. Cattle are grazing near Mt. San Antonio. Fields broaden out along the hills of Brea Canyon.

City of Industry has small industries along the boulevard, but your view is mostly open and you do not feel constricted. After passing under 605 Freeway, turn southwestward on Durfee Avenue. City of Industry is gone, and you are bicycling past Whittier Narrows Nature Center and Wildlife Sanctuary. A new area leads into Legg Lake Park of the Whittier Narrows Dam Recreation Area. The lake was unrippled for us in the afternoon stillness. Durfee becomes San Gabriel Boulevard. Pedal north to Mission Boulevard and Mission San Gabriel Archangel.

No bells will peal, but how often have you had this kind of a trip from Riverside? The biking distance is an easy 63 miles.

Legg Lake, between Riverside and San Gabriel, "was unrippled for us in the afternoon stillness. . . . ."

VII.
Mission Interlude

Back in the 1960s, Russ Leadabrand wrote in his evocative *Westway* Magazine series, later compiled into a book—*Exploring California Byways in and around Los Angeles*: "There was a time when the major tourist attractions of Southern California were grouped inland of Los Angeles in a corner of country you could roughly call the West San Gabriel Valley. In their own way and time as famous as Disneyland is now were the Mt. Lowe Railway, the Cawston Ostrich Farm, Gay's Lion Farm . . . All are gone now . . . yet the gentle death of these landmarks in no way signaled the end of the scenic attractions of San Gabriel Valley."

You realize the truth of this observation as you bicycle into the civic center of San Gabriel and the environs of too-seldom-visited San Gabriel Mission.

The architecture of the civic center blends gracefully with the old Mission that still stands like a bastion along El Camino Real. A blue line drawn on the sidewalk leads you around Paseo Historico. It is a walk through the early history of California, a meeting with the names of historic families now virtually unknown. Site of City Hall was donated by Walter P. Temple, whose grandfather traveled around the horn to Los Angeles in 1841, when some of the small children of the Anza expedition must still have been

Father Font thoroughly approved of Mission San Gabriel, including the Indians. He found some "five hundred souls, recently converted" living in a compound of huts around the Mission. There was no sign of possible repercussions from the San Diego uprising. "The converted Indians," he wrote, "appear to be gentle, friendly and of good hearts." He also approved of efforts being made "to have the matured, unmarried girls sleep apart in some privacy."

"The method which the Fathers observe in the conversion," he chronicled, "is not to oblige anyone to become a Christian, admitting only those who voluntarily offer themselves, and they do this in the following manner: Since these Indians are accustomed to live in the fields and hills like beasts, the Fathers require that if they wish to become Christians they shall no longer go to the forest, but must live in the Mission; and if they leave the rancheria, as they call the little village of huts and houses, they will go seek them and will punish them. . . ."

Each day started with Mass. Font felt so much better that he not only helped to say Mass, but provided the musical accompaniment on an instrument he had carried for long months on the trail. It was a psaltery, the classic musical instrument consisting of a flat sounding-box with numerous strings which he plucked skillfully, wincing a little because some of the other padres "did not have good voices."

The Indians participated in the Mass, the communal breakfast of *atole,* the noon meal of *pozole.* They were the beginning of the work force that was to make Mission wealthy.

alive. His great-grandfather on his mother's side of the family—William Workman—organized with James Rowland the first wagon train to Southern California from Independence, Missouri. The Temples opened the first mercantile store in Los Angeles. The Temple-Workman families founded Temple City. A great grandson became historian of Mission San Gabriel. Close to City Hall steps is a millstone commemorating the Chapman Mill, built in 1823 by Joseph Chapman, once captured as a "pirate" by Spanish warships trying to hold an empire whose furthest outreach on the Pacific Coast had been established by Juan Bautista de Anza.

Lopez Adobe behind the Mission was completed about 1806, and now houses a collection of historical California photographs. Legend blends amiably with history along this Blue Line Walk. The Old Grapevine is supposed to have come from the garden of "Ramona's home", held by romantic tradition to be the birthplace of the heroine of Helen Hunt Jackson's novel.

Plaza Park, in fact not fancy, was the original stage for the world-famous Mission Play, presented here by John Steven McGroarty from 1912 to 1927. McGroarty also had the versatility to become a two-term member of the U.S. Congress and poet laureate of California. Mission Play-house in the present Civic Auditorium was opened in 1927 to take over production of the Mission Play. Opening night was a gala occasion for the socially prominent of Southern California. King Alfonso of Spain contributed the wall hangings, still in the auditorium. Congressman-Poet Laureate McGroarty inspired Vic, the town barber for 35 years, to open El Poche Cafe as an adjunct to the barbering business. El Poche, a block off the Blue Line today, is perhaps the most historic and least-publicized Mexican restaurant in Southern California. It undoubtedly has one of the finest kitchens, and local citizens make the same claim for Panchito's on Mission Drive. Close to the entrance of El Poche's Rincon Flamenco Tower, with its

67

Mission San Gabriel, fourth among the California Missions, had been founded in 1771, only two years after the discovery of San Gabriel Valley. Font described the surrounding valley as having an abundance of live oaks. Celery, parsnips, turnips and watercress grew with minimal care along the creek:

"The Mission has such fine advantages for crops and such good pastures for cattle and horses that nothing better could be desired. The cows which they have are fat and they give much and rich milk, with which they make cheese and very good butter. They raise hogs and have a small flock of sheep, of which on our arrival they killed three or four. Their flesh was especially good, and I do not remember having eaten fatter or finer mutton. . . ."

The aches and chills of Coyote Canyon seemed far behind.

Commando Don Fernando from Monterey wanted Anza and part of his troops to help him deal with the uprising in San Diego, and if "possible to capture the prime movers of the rebellion, and to administer to them punishment appropriate to their assault, as well as to others who merit it."

Anza agreed to go, and his colonists were more than content to wait for him in San Gabriel. They could easily have been persuaded to settle here for the rest of their lives.

Anza also decided to let Father Font continue his recuperation at the Mission, but made the mistake of not first discussing the decision with him. . . .

graceful curving staircase, is an oak wine cask from the old San Gabriel winery, among the largest in the world in the 1880s. Wine-making started with the canny padres of the Mission.

Father Font's shrewd assessment of Mission San Gabriel was substantiated by history. After the first few years of struggle to survive, the Mission was a wealth of grapes, oranges, olives. A traveler wrote of "cattle on a thousand hills." San Gabriel helped to supply later Missions, produced food, soap, candle wax, hides for surrounding communities and passing traders. For more than a century and a half, it was on the high road of commercial and religious traffic. Improbably, the first ship built in California—a 99-ton sail schooner, was constructed here at the Mission, then dismantled and carted to the roadstead of San Pedro. Even more improbable is the fact that the ship was built—in association with a Michael White and Mission Indians—by the "pirate" Joseph Chapman.

Though it doesn't have the swallows and the tourists of Mission San Juan Capistrano, San Gabriel Mission is architecturally unique. The present church, built between 1791 and 1805, was designed by Father Antonio Cruzado, a Spanish priest born and raised in Cordova. Moorish influence is evidenced by the buttressed walls, vaulted roof and fortress walls more than four feet thick. A bell on the street corner marks El Camino Real, the King's Highway that connected all the Missions in California and was the main route of communication from South to North. The main altar was brought from Mexico City in the 1790s. In the sanctuary is a 300-year-old painting, "Our Lady of Sorrows." The Museum, in a building constructed in 1812, has a collection of paintings by Indians of the fourteen stations of the Cross, probably the oldest Indian sacred art in California. Colors were made from wild flowers; olive oil was the base. One of the books in the literature room was published in 1489. The rosewood organ came from France in 1821. Campo Santo within the Mission walls is the 69

When the commander came personally to communicate his decision, Font blew his new-found cool:

"I replied that it was very hard that I should be the last to know of his decisions with regard to halting or marching, and that he never took me into account for anything, although I had said to him before leaving San Miguel before we set out that during the whole journey I should not leave his side, but since it was his wish to leave me here, I would abide by his decision and would have patience, as I had done on other occasions. . . . I was only causing him hindrance and trouble anyway, and he would do well to leave me behind in order to free himself of such rubbish. . . ."

Font added: "The commander tried to mollify me as best he could . . . Thereupon, we two alone engaged in a long conversation. It was in terms of friendship and peace, but I spoke to him very plainly. . . ."

Anzà then invited Father Font to accompany him to San Diego, and to "carry the quadrant to observe the latitude of that port."

The latitude of San Diego had been known to mariners for more than a century, but Father Font promptly gave up the comforts of San Gabriel to accompany the military expedition southward.

"I note this all down," he wrote, "in order that it may be seen that with such gentlemen it is well to speak plainly when the occasion arises. . . ."

oldest cemetery in Los Angeles County, consecrated in 1778. It is really two levels of cemetery. Beneath the present tombstones are the graves of 6,000 Indians, most of whom died during the cholera and smallpox epidemic of 1825. The fountain in the garden splashes playfully. When a group of students from nearby Azusa toured the Mission in the early autumn of 1975, one student reported that Senor Lupido—his great-grandfather still alive at age 102—had in youth sculptured the lion's head on the fountain, through which the water flows. We found San Gabriel Mission to be an active contemporary church, deeply involved under Clarentian Father Leo in a "campaign for human development," and community programs "to meet immediate human needs."

Taking off along the Anza trail from here can be one of the most agreeable walks or short bike rides in Southern California.

Go around behind the Mission and start up Santa Anita Street, past the Mission High School and Hospital. Santa Anita will phase into San Marino Drive. Continue up this Drive toward the mountains, passing fine old homes that speak of another age in Southern California. At Stratford Road, a Huntington Library direction sign will guide you one long block west to the 200 acres around the Henry E. Huntington Library and Art Gallery. Besides the treasures of the library and gallery, which can be studied on tours guided by docents, there are a collection of 25,000 desert plants, the Oriental Gardens and Southern California's first avocado grove. You may even decide to weekend at Henry E.'s hotel, now the Huntington-Sheraton.

Your walk or bicycle ride continues up Orlando along the Huntington estate grounds. Wend west on Cameron Drive and Arden Road, then north on Wilson to California Street, about a mile from the Pasadena Freeway. Exclusive of your ramblings through the Huntington estate, you've traversed just five miles since leaving Mission San Gabriel.

The expedition to San Diego added another dimension to the personal and historic drama of the Anza expedition. Captain Rivera proved to be a devious man, paranoic, extremely jealous. He had been looking forward to Anza's arrival in Monterey with more than mixed feelings, and now the rebellion in San Diego gave him a windfall chance to delay and perhaps to sidetrack it. Father Font's perceptive eye probed quickly to the heart of the matter: After the founding of the Presidio at Monterey, Rivera had explored the San Francisco peninsula and reported to Mexico City that it offered little possibility for future settlement. As Commandant in California, he now felt he could save face by having Anza deliver the settlers to him in Southern California; at a later date, he could take a second look at the San Francisco peninsula and then found the settlement at a place of his own discovery.

Anza, however, believed he should hold to the Viceroy's instructions and deliver the expedition at least to Monterey. In a stern and fatherly manner, Font counseled him to persevere on this course. When Font became ill again in San Diego, Rivera showed great concern and tried to split him off from Anza by urging that he remain on the South Coast instead of endangering his health by traveling any further to the north. Emissaries began to suggest that Font remain. Finally he told them all with characteristic acerbity: "Spare your pains, Gentlemen; I have no intention of remaining here."

Anza also was unhappy with Rivera's handling of the investigation into the uprising. Indians were arrested, some were beaten, one died as a result of the beating, but Anza could see no orderly plan or objective. He decided to return to San Gabriel, but diplomatically gave Rivera a chance to save face on the issue of a San Francisco settlement: Should there be no suitable site near the port, perhaps one could be found a short distance from it. Font reported that Rivera then said, "Well, friend, go ahead, go ahead..."

But he meant, "Not too far ahead," as Anza and Father Font were soon to learn.

"...though it doesn't have swallows, San Gabriel Mission is architecturally unique..."

73

Anza left a dozen soldiers and their families to strengthen San Gabriel Mission against possible future trouble with the Indians. The march to Monterey was resumed again on Wednesday, February 21, 1776. On the East Coast, a new flag with red and white stripes was being flown over the Continental Army headquarters of General George Washington. Father Font not only said Mass before the expedition started, but also pronounced a blessing with ashes, then settled into his sermon: "With the gospel of the day, I confirmed all that from the beginning of the journey I had said to them in the talks which I had made to them. . . . ." The march didn't get under way until 11:30 A.M. On the route toward what was to be Glendale, the expedition crossed Los Angeles River. Font wrote that the river carried "a great deal of water," and that the land "was very green and flower-strewn." During the next day's march to Calabasas and the camp at Las Virgenes Creek, Font found San Fernando Valley to be "plentiful with live oaks." He also saw "some heathen, although few, and these naked and unarmed."

VIII.
Glendale to Calabasas

As we paused at the surging intersection of California Street and Arroyo Parkway, and watched the traffic streaming to and from the Pasadena Freeway, the route immediately ahead seemed to pose far more problems for a quiet passage in 1976 than it did for Anza in 1776. By automobile, the shortest way westward would be out Colorado Boulevard and into the Ventura Freeway, crossing en route the Golden State Freeway, the Hollywood Freeway and the San Diego Freeway. But what about a safe, let alone a pleasant, way to proceed by bicycle?

For awhile, it didn't appear we'd be able to approximate anything like our bike trail from Riverside to San Gabriel. However, as we probed tentatively along, a path of relative tranquility across the central San Fernando Valley began to look plausible.

To get near Anza's Glendale campsite by bicycle, we continued west on California Street to Orange Grove, then turned northward along Orange Grove to Colorado Boulevard, passing the old mansion that houses the Tournament of Roses headquarters. The route of the Rose Parade is along this section of Orange Grove. The street is wide. What were once private mansions along the way are becoming segmented into apartments, but on a Sunday

Horsey country "just a few droppings from downtown Burbank . . ."

morning you have a feeling of what Pasadena must have been like before World War II.

Staying below the freeway, follow Colorado Boulevard and Colorado Street to Glendale Avenue. The avenue will take you south to the ending of Las Feliz Boulevard near the main entrance to Forest Lawn Cemetery, which is perhaps more tranquility than you'd care to integrate into your personal Anza trail re-enactment.

Starting anew from where Las Feliz Boulevard resurrects itself beneath the long shadow of the hilltop cross at Forest Lawn, we bicycled westward to Riverside Drive, and here turned north into the lush greenery, golf fairways and horsetrails of Griffith Park. There are picnic grounds for resting in the park. A blinking light warns you to watch for horses crossing the street. Riverside and Zoo Drive weave a linking trail. The hills beneath which Anza camped can be etched clear against the sky, when the sky is clear of smog as it happily was for us. At the northern limits of the park, you are cycling through an island of horsey country that seems an impossible anachronism so close to two freeways. Equestre Inn and Pickwick Stables are just a few droppings from downtown Burbank. Part of this is a marked bicycle route shaded by maples.

Follow Riverside Drive along Tolucca Lake's small restaurant row, from the Irish Knight to Alfonse's. Swerve left on Moorpark and on into Lankershim past Universal City. Pick up Ventura Boulevard just under the Hollywood Freeway.

Bicycling Ventura Boulevard on a Sunday morning is to have leisure and safety, a seeming remoteness from freeway traffic, as you pass through Studio City, Sherman Oaks, Encino, Tarzana, Woodland Hills.

Another restaurant row takes form, and you pass them slowly enough for the names to fashion their own fantasy verse: St. Moritz, Hayloft, Sportsman's, McHenry's, Barone's ... Casting Office, Copper Penny, Benihana, Ram's Horn, Valle Forge, Travaglini's ... Hangman's Tree, 77

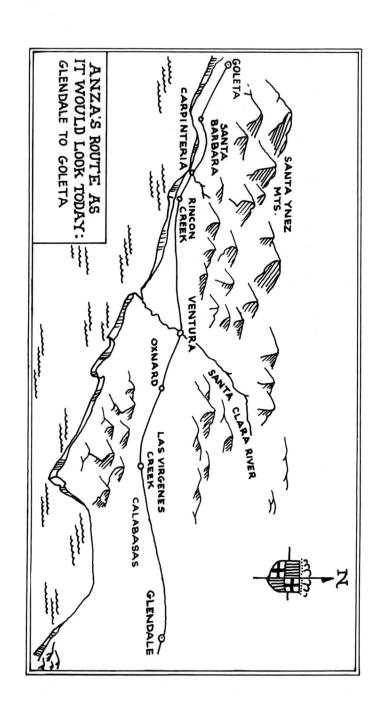

ANZA'S ROUTE AS
IT WOULD LOOK TODAY:
GLENDALE TO GOLETA

GOLETA

SANTA
BARBARA

CARPINTERIA

SANTA YNEZ
MTS.

RINCON
CREEK

VENTURA

OXNARD

SANTA CLARA RIVER

LAS VIRGENES
CREEK

CALABASAS

GLENDALE

N

Ritzi Rib, Rassmatazz and just plain old Charlie Brown's. . . .

Churches, temples, water bed emporiums and a good deal of rather pleasant middle class funk are scattered between the inventively named restaurants.

Gradually, Ventura Boulevard begins to phase into open country. Victoria Station, featuring prime rib, shares a stretch of it with the impressive arches and glasswork of the Jehovah Witness Assembly Hall.

Turn briefly up Topanga Canyon Boulevard, then right or west into Avenue San Luis. Willows and eucalyptus shade comfortable hillside homes.

And suddenly you are into the unexpected charm of Old Calabasas, having negotiated the San Fernando portion of the De Anza trail without trauma. From Glendale to Old Calabasas clocks out as a 30-mile bike ride, tailor perfect for an early Sunday morning start.

Friday, February 23, 1776 was the last day of the journey to the coastal route along the South Sea. Anza and the future freeway builders evidently chose the same terrain. Font reported a long grade, followed by a relatively easy descent, "from which one sees the sea and the first islands of the Channel of Santa Barbara." The same road today would be through Russell Valley, past Newberry Park, and down Conejo Grade to Camarillo and the Santa Clara River.

Beyond the Conejo Grade, the expedition passed four small Indian villages, then a herd of antelope. Father Font became poetic again: "We saw in the plain a very large drove of antelopes which, as soon as they saw us, fled like the wind, looking like a cloud skimming along the earth."

Concerning the Indians, Font reported that all "were unarmed and naked." The women, he added, "were very cautious and hardly a one left their huts, because the soldiers of Monterey, since they were not married, had offended them with various excesses which the unbridling of their passions caused them to commit. . . . ."

Santa Clara River charmed Font with a profusion of "geese, duck, cranes and other fowl."

"At sunset," he wrote, "a very thick fog arose from the sea, with which the day ended very much clouded over, and the night was very dark. This matter of the fog is very common and continuous along these coasts, but it is not injurious."

IX.

Calabasas to the sea

The sign on Calabasas Road says "Welcome to Old Calabasas." It's a western welcome to a small pocket of countryside that has been trying against considerable odds to preserve and recreate something of a vanished West. Ventura Freeway 101 is scarcely a mile to the north. Motorists rocketing along it seldom slow down enough to have a wonder about Old Calabasas.

The Leonis adobe on the main street of Calabasas is part of a ranch that began working cattle in 1844. It has been saved almost intact with wagons, white wooden balcony and windmill for pumping water, and is open to the public from 1 to 4 P.M. Wednesdays, Saturdays and Sundays. The spread is "Privately maintained: Donations appreciated, but not required."

Directly across the street is a boardwalk strung with wooden storefronts that house the Clay Pot, Handwrought Jewelry, Ladybug Antiques and a little boutique called the Diplomat. Not western, but amiable.

Las Virgenes Enterprise, one of two sharply professional weeklies serving this area, occupies a frame cottage on the boardwalk. *Las Virginese Independent* is the other paper that helped to orient two cyclists to this section of the Anza trail. We learned that when a fire started in the home of the Oscar Grubwieser family, all the neighbors turned

81

"...motorists rocketing along the freeway will never slow down enough to have a wonder about Old Calabasas...."

82

out in a vain effort to save it—while waiting for a Fire Department truck that didn't arrive for thirty minutes. Page 2 of the *Independent* was divided with meticulous journalistic fairness into a "Right Side" and a leftish side. The name of the "On The Right Side" columnist was an inspired choice: Theodore Roosevelt Sorensen. TRS was outraged by liberals of the effete eastern news media; he is certain they are conspiring to set up our "motherland" for easy conquest by the Soviets and the Chinese—by trying simultaneously to take away our pistols and whittle down the Pentagon budget. The liberals would then have the opportunity to rebuild America out of the ashes into their own kind of country, after a suitable period during which we would be forced to "grovel and do penance before the Third World." It was a vision of Armageddon that could well bring Teddy himself threshing out of the grave, in search of a pistol and a horse. On the left side of the page, a columnist more prosaically named H. James Horwitz was equally outraged by a report that former President Richard Nixon was going to net at least $2,650,000 from his autobiography and the taped TV sessions with David Frost. "How," demanded H. James Horwitz, "can you teach children not to lie and steal?"

Gas lights stand along the Old Calabasas boardwalk. Sagebrush Cantina serves Mexican food, and has outdoor patio tables for sunny days.

Ventura Freeway doesn't leave many options for bicyclists and walkers who might want to follow the Anza trail. Back in 1969, while bicycling from San Francisco to Los Angeles, I avoided having to deal with the problem by biking from Santa Barbara through Ojai and across Simi Valley. But this is too far to the north of the Anza route.

The only other possibility is to stay just south of Ventura Freeway and follow the winding grades of Mulholland Highway, then Potrero Road, along the crest of the Santa Monica Mountains. This route takes you near the Anza camp at Las Virgenes Creek, the expedition's

From Calabasas to the sea: " . . .on a weekend morning this was a road of solitude. . . ."

only stop between the mountains west of Glendale and the Pacific coast.

We now had to make the same kind of decision forced upon us by the elements at Coyote Canyon. The trip through the Santa Monica Mountains would be about 50 miles from Calabasas to the sea, with a number of severe grades. It would be too long and too demanding a bicycle day for Elfriede. She would drive the route with Zorba, our Hungarian sheepdog protector, and we'd meet at the coast.

From Calabasas, you gear up a rather easy grade for a mile along Mulholland Drive, then turn west into Mulholland Highway. The world "highway" is more than somewhat a misnomer. Once you are beyond Calabasas High School, the road is two quiet lanes winding along peaceful hillsides. A sign warned me to watch out for deer the next six miles. A horse looked up from a trough that had been contrived from a white enamel bathtub. On a weekend morning this was a road of solitude. A house of striking contemporary design, made of natural wood, stood alone on its own hill. The farming and cattle valley was pure shangrila. A herd of black cattle watched me pass by with that special look of devotion a cyclist can expect only from cows. At Las Virgines Road, where horses instead of cows were grazing, Mulholland begins a two-mile ascent. Unless you are a purist, you may decide—as I did—to get off and push your bike for awhile. When you're working too hard to climb a grade, you really can't appreciate the translucense of a butterfly's wings. From the summit, you coast down into a valley of ranches. You have a feeling that both Anza and Father Font would be pleased at the way this countryside has survived two centuries.

At Cornell Road, detour down Lake Vista Drive for a half-mile or so to Malibu Club Lake. I didn't know what was there, but still the temptation was too much. A sailboat promptly paid off the extra mile by drifting across the small lake for me. Malibu Club is one of those private

" . . Los Angeles is behind, the sea somewhere ahead beyond the quiet mountain lake. . . . ."

enclaves that can go almost unnoticed in Southern California. In 1922, it was incorporated as a private club for "recreation and social enjoyment" by Cecil B. DeMille and other legendary names of legendary Hollywood. The club has a 44-acre jewel of a lake set in 240 acres of tree-covered mountains. "Pleasant personality and gregarious attitudes" are two qualifications for membership. Others include the resources and contacts to acquire a piece of club property, and then to lay down a comparatively modest front-money membership fee of $1,000. After that, you are free to be pleasant and gregarious, and to enjoy sunrise and sunset bracketed around a 45-minute drive to downtown Los Angeles.

Back on Mulholland, "The Old Place" at Troutdale Road intrigued me with antlers over the entrance and an offer of wine, steak and clams. Since this wasn't a good midday biking diet, I went right on by—but we will return.

Leaving Cornell, there's another walk, push and watch-the-butterfly wings grade. Magnificent rock formations rise like turrets on the hilltops, guarding the valley far below. Turn right, or northward, off Mulholland onto what is—at this point—grandiosely called Westlake Boulevard. The road is narrow, the downgrade wearing on your hand-brakes, but the view of the mountains and the canyons is superb.

Veer west again on Potrero Road toward Lake Sherwood and Hidden Valley country. Another sailboat obligingly was waiting for my camera, riffling a sunlit mirror. There was still another warning at the end of the lake to be considerate of passing deer. The lake slowly surrendered the landscape to the gnarled trees and white fences of New England countryside. The road became level and beautifully straight across wide pasturelands cradled between hills. Adolph's Hidden Valley Ranch offered "equitation," which probably is not another form of TM. Royal Oaks seems to specialize in thorobred horses. Sisters of Notre Dame Convent is cloistered behind eucalyptus trees, and the air is breathing air.

. . . from Calabasas to the sea.

Within a half-dozen miles after the Reino Road turnoff to Newbury Park, Potrero's long, level peacefulness hairpins down toward the sea—and suddenly there is a vista of the Pacific Ocean, Anza's South Sea, almost as welcome to me as it was to Anza, Father Font and flock.

Down at sea level, a lemon grove breaks the checkerboard greenery of the fields. Those mountaintops that seem to be just ahead aren't another coastal range to be crossed. They are the crests of the Santa Barbara Islands, far out in the channel.

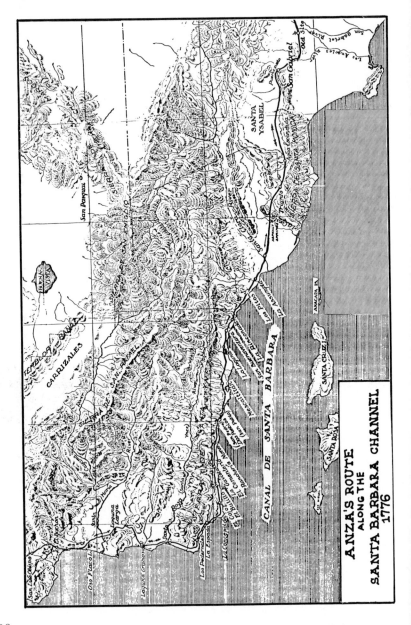

ANZA'S ROUTE
ALONG THE
SANTA BARBARA CHANNEL
1776

X.
Port Hueneme to Goleta

If Juan Bautista de Anza had to deal with the Commandant of Alta California after reaching the South Sea, we knew from past encounters that we would now have to contend with the Alta California Highway Patrol, the U.S. military and local police—not to mention various public and private quasi-laws—in trying to follow the old Mission Trail by any means other than mechanized horsepower.

The biking and walking route ahead was our own camino-not-quite-so-real. Four years earlier, in July and August of 1971, we had walked along here together for 26 days, from Los Angeles to San Francisco. No historian has yet shown me that Elfriede is not the only woman in history to have walked this route. Anza's pioneer women had saddle horses for breathers. Indian migrations over such a distance could have taken decades. When in 1969 I had put together a bicycle trail from San Francisco to Los Angeles, then unknowingly following much of the Anza trail in reverse, Elfriede had driven a support car with our gear to nightly meeting places. In neither of these trips had we attempted to round Point Conception by land, the route of the 1776 Anza expedition.

Bicycling down past Camarillo State Hospital, the trail from Calabasas led quickly into Hueneme Road, across

"...phone ahead to reserve the sewing machine for two..."

fields of tomatoes, spinach, beans and groves of lemon trees. Elfriede, the support car and Zorba were waiting in front of Port Hueneme's Missile Motel. Though we didn't intend to overnight there, we were happy to see it hadn't succumbed either to progress or recession. When we had reached it the first time after walking 26.5 miles from Point Dume, it had been just about at the outer limit of our range for that day. Our evening meal in the cafe with the pool table had seemed a princely banquet. We shared the Missile that night with Mexican-American beanfield workers who offered to help us find jobs.

With bicycles, your range is greatly extended, and there's no problem going on to more comfortable—though not more friendly—accommodations at Ventura Marina. Follow Hueneme Road to Ventura Road, which still has a shady blacktop path along the Seabee residential area. Channel Islands Boulevard, Victoria Avenue, 5th Street and Harbor Boulevard will take you without urban stress into Marina Plaza.

There at the waterfront this time, we were rewarded with the discovery of John's at the Beach, a seafood restaurant to be noted for your own coastal travels. John Blonder started putting it together after studying art in Paris and Barcelona. The resultant collage is a fish shanty here, a barrel there, an old sewing machine where it seems to function best as a table. You can actually phone ahead to reserve the sewing machine for two.

Ventura itself, only 69 miles up the coast from Los Angeles, is too often bypassed by motorists passing along the freeway. Afoot or by bicycle, you have to stop. The Visitor's Bureau, just up Seaward Avenue from John Blonder's sewing machine, dispenses do-it-yourself mini guides to a range of attractions from old San Buenaventura Mission and Olivas Adobe to the Potter's Guild, poetry readings, the Handweaver's Guild, sportfishing and sailing, the Cabrillo Music Theater, Master Chorale and a full symphony.

93

Anza's diary for February 24, 1776, noted that the expedition left the Santa Clara River camp at 9 A.M., "with a dense fog and signs of rain." He went on:

"In a little more than six hours we traveled four leagues, and at three o'clock in the afternoon we came to the Rancherias del Rincon, where a halt was made for the night. In this village we found an abundance of good fish, some of which it has been estimated are more than a foot long, exclusive of the tail. . ."

Font's diary gives more of a feeling of the march:

"All this road as far as the camp site runs along the sea beach, almost touching the waves. For this reason it is a very diverting way, and it would have been more so if the weather had been good. The people of the expedition who had never seen the sea found many things to marvel at. . . ."

The Indians of the Santa Barbara Channel were the largest tribe Font had seen since leaving the Yuma nation. The total population had been estimated at around 20,000. Some villages exceeded "a thousand souls." Their houses were even better than those of the Yumas—"round in form, like a half orange, very spacious, large and high."

Communal life was rather sophisticated:

"They have a common temescal. This is a hot, closed room for sweating, made somewhat subterranean and very firm with poles and earth, and having at the top, in the middle, an opening like a scuttle, to afford air and to serve as a door, through which they go down inside by a ladder. I peeped into a temescal and perceived a strong heat coming from it. In the middle of them they make a fire. The Indians enter to perspire, seated all around, and as soon as they perspire freely and wet the ground with their sweat, they run out and jump into the sea to bathe themselves. . . ."

From Seaward Avenue, follow the bike path and promenade along the harbor, past San Buenaventura State Park. Turn up California to see, on its own hill, the period piece in white architecture that is City Hall. You get the same sort of visual impact by turning up Figueroa toward the Mission.

It was no fault of Father Serra's that there wasn't a Mission here in 1776 to welcome Anza and his colonists. Serra had planned for a Mission as early as 1768. It was to have been the third in Alta California, an anchor point between San Diego and Monterey, but the Viceroy judged there wouldn't be enough soldiers to protect the intermediate site. Three other Missions were founded at safer locations. In 1773, when Serra was age 60 and partially crippled, he returned to Mexico City to plead the case of San Buenaventura. Finally, in 1782, a cavalcade left San Gabriel with church goods for the new Mission. Father Serra managed to be on hand on Easter Sunday to sing the first Mass. San Buenaventura's acqueduct system made its rancho lands among the richest in California, yet the Mission itself was not to be wealthy for long. After independence from Spain, Mexico began turning over the Mission lands to great landed families that enjoyed their own brief Golden Age of California. During the U.S. war of conquest, John C. Fremont's men fired only two shots to drive the last Mexican defender, Don Jose Amaz, from the Mission. Since 1840, San Buenaventura has been a parish church. In the Depression years of the 1930s, it became a refuge for the jobless and homeless wandering along the coast. We stopped and rested here during our coastal trek in 1971.

As you pause in Ventura along the Anza trail, and follow the street signs with their distinctive mission-style lettering, even the sailboats in the marina, their sails as bright and graceful as a seagull's wing in the morning sun, will have a long link with the past. This was a coast of seagoing people a bicentennial before Father Font marvel-

"...turning up Figueroa toward old San Buenaventura Mission...."

led at the Indian canoes. Cabrillo sailed along here in 1542, just fifty years after the first voyage of Columbus, and was amazed by the fleets of swift sea-going canoes. He called Ventura "Pueblo de las Canoas." Olivas Adobe is another historical thread weaving through the heritage of this coast. Don Raimundo Olivas was born in Los Angeles scarcely a quarter of a century after Anza led his people westward from San Gabriel. The Olivas were one of only seventy families in Los Angeles, among them such familiar names of today as Figueroa, Pico and Sepulveda. Don Raimundo, through family friendship with an Indian woman, received information that helped to prevent a planned attack on Mission San Buenaventura. When the lands were secularized, he received a grant of almost 5,000 acres and built the balconied Monterey style home that still receives visitors.

The Big Greenhouse is a heritage home that may be of more pragmatic interest to the Anza trail follower arriving in Ventura near the dinner hour. The style of this home is Victorian rather than Monterey. Textured wall covering, an oval stained glass skylight, shimmering crystal completed the setting for our one-menu family dinner: A tureen of soup, platters of *both* charbroiled steak and fried chicken, hot cornbread and honey, a whole chocolate cake, margaritas by the pitcher-full. Bikers and hikers of the world do need to sustain the spirit. It helps that the Big Greenhouse is on the corner of the promenade leading up to Mission San Buenaventura.

Weave your way on up Main Street to 101 Freeway. Bicyclists have to break the law mildly to pedal up the ramp and ride the safe shoulder. This is the only bicycle way to the north; two bikers from Carpenteria told us that here we wouldn't be hassled by the police. This was tacitly confirmed at the next "State Beaches" offramp, where a freeway marker confirms your presence by advising: "Bicycles must exit." A sign of the slowly changing times along California highways.

Font's eye of a novelist allows us to see the Channel Indians as he saw them:

"They are well formed and of good body, although not very corpulent, on account of their sweating, I judge. The women are fairly goodlooking. They wear pendants in their ears, and have their front hair short and banged, the rest falling over their shoulders. . . .

"The dress of the men is usually total nakedness. For adornment only they are in the habit of wearing around the waist a string or other geegaw which covers nothing . . . The women cover themselves with a deerskin hung around the waist, and with some sort of beaver skin cape over their backs . . . They seem to live without law or king, and especially without knowledge of God, so far as I was able to ascertain. . . ."

Font was most intrigued with the skill of the Channel Indians in boat building, fishing and navigating. He gives history's best account:

"They are great fishermen and very ingenous. Above all, they build launches with which they navigate. They are very carefully made of several planks which they work with no tools than their shells and flints. They join them at the seams by sewing them with very strong thread, and fit the joints with pitch, by which they are made very strong and secure. Some of the launches are decorated with little shells and all are painted red with hematite . . . They carry poles which end in blades, these being oars with which they row alternately, now on one side and now on the other side of the launch. In this way they guide the launch wherever they wish, sailing through rough seas with much boldness. . ."

Father Font met one Indian who had just come across the channel from Santa Cruz Island.

After exiting, ride the old beach road along the rippling surf, past a succession of state and county beaches. Hangkite gliders soar off the cliffs above you to land among the surfers on the beach. At Seacliff, you bike up on the freeway again, ignoring the old sign banning bicycles, pedestrians and horses. Don't be too concerned about being arrested; the freeway ends in a mile at Rincon Cliff House, close to Anza's Rincon Creek campsite. Walking the coast four years earlier, we overnighted at the simple but comfortable Cliff House. With a bicycle, it's only a 35-mile day to go on into Montecito and Santa Barbara. Turn off 101 in Carpenteria and pedal pleasantly along Via Real, Lillie and Ortega Hill roads, passing a polo field.

To bicycle and walk through Santa Barbara is always one of the loveliest days of a coastal trip. Those "Yield to Pedestrians" signs on bicycle paths are beautiful to behold. From Coast Village Road in Montecito, turn toward the ocean on Cabrillo to travel through Audree Clark Bird Refuge and watch the white geese making trails on the sheltered lake. Follow Cabrillo, Shoreline Drive, Cliff Drive and Marina Drive along the ocean. Roble Road and Las Palmas wind you away from the beach through the horsey tranquility of Hope Ranch Estates. Leave Laguna Blanca and La Cumbre Country Club at Via Presada. Then let Via Tranquilla and Nogal Road take you up to Hollister Avenue in Goleta. This is a part of the Anza trail not to be forgotten.

You will be tempted to linger at many places in and around Santa Barbara, which can claim without too much debate to be the most liveable city along the Southern California coast. To check the "What's Happening in Santa Barbara" calendar for any given month is to want to stay in town for a month. In one representative month of 1975, no less than sixty-eight events were scheduled. Should you not have chosen to become involved with the poet Toby Lurie, who uses chants and mantras to involve his 99

The Indian women ran and hid as Anza's people came close to their villages. Font investigated. Men blocked the doors whenever he went near a hut:

"I went up to a door, and although I did not ask permission to go in, knowing their dislike for it, nevertheless two minutes could not have passed when they shut the inner door on me and I withdrew unenlightened. . ."

Font got a clue when the Indians kept asking if "Comacho was coming. . ."

Comacho, Font learned, was the name given by the Indians to one of the worst of the Monterey soldiers who had traveled up the coast. He raped so many women that the Indians took to calling every soldier *Comacho*.

"This is all the result," Font wrote, "of the extortions and outrages which the soldiers perpetrated when in their journeys they passed along the Channel, especially in the beginning.

The whirlwind of revenge, which Father Serra had warned would come, was slowly building in Alta California.

Along the beach north of Ventura.

In Audree Clark Bird Refuge, Santa Barbara: "...watching geese make trails on the lake..."

102

audience, you could have spent an evening with Soviet violinist Irina Bochkova—or at a University of California Santa Barbara campus lecture on "The Selling of Foreign Aid." Isla Vista near the campus is no longer the storm and tumult of the late 1960s; contemporary concerns are expressed in more subtle ways.

Santa Barbara Mission wasn't founded until 1786, a decade after Anza and Father Font rode near its present site, and two years after the death of Father Serra. For the Anza Re-enactment Committee's ride and program, Father Geiger and Father Virgil agreed to represent the Mission at the Goleta campground ceremonies. They would read from Father Font's diary and deliver the invocation, but definitely would not climb on a horse. "I'm 75," said Father Geiger, Mission historian, "and my backside is too historical."

For a cyclist or a walker traveling the Anza trail, it's best to stay overnight in Goleta for an early start along the coast the next morning. For our own Anza travels, we picked the Pepper Tree Inn, fortuitously next to Chuck's of Hawaii Steak House. A reader of our *Los Angeles* Magazine column believes that no one should stay anywhere in Santa Barbara except at the Biltmore: ". . . .like Del Monte Lodge in Monterey, one of the last of its kind in first-class hotels. . . ." With remarkable objectivity, the Biltmore has described its La Marina Dining Room —Andalusian decor and architecture overlooking the Pacific—as "the second best restaurant in Santa Barbara." The first was conceded to be the Talk of the Town, in a New England setting.

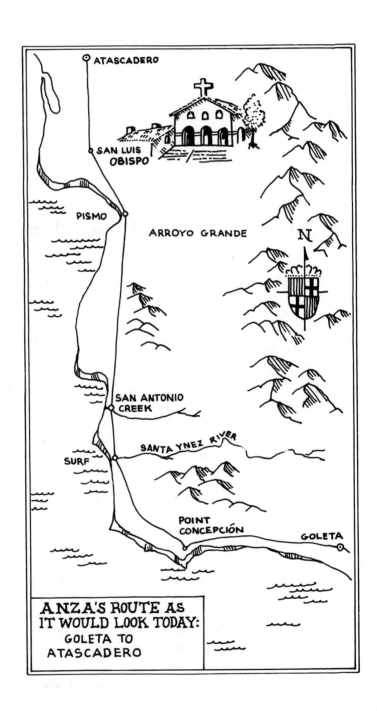

ATASCADERO

SAN LUIS OBISPO

PISMO

ARROYO GRANDE

N

SAN ANTONIO CREEK

SURF

SANTA YNEZ RIVER

POINT CONCEPCIÓN

GOLETA

ANZA'S ROUTE AS
IT WOULD LOOK TODAY:
GOLETA TO
ATASCADERO

XI.
Trespassing Point Conception

Anza, Father Font, Father Junipero Serra and Jesus himself would have to carry bail money to round Point Conception by land today.

Jesus might make it by walking on water here and there, although the Pacific Ocean along this rugged coast looks less receptive to miracles than the Sea of Galilee.

I know of no other historic trail on earth that has been so effectively closed to the public.

"Thou Shalt Not Trespass" has become here the 11th Commandment, writ as if on a tablet of stone by the State of California freeway system, the Southern Pacific Railroad, two vast private ranches and Vandenberg Air Force Base.

Anza Re-enactment Committee riders had to get special one-time permission to approximate a portion of the trail by riding across private ranchlands otherwise closed to the public.

By automobile or a freeway-approved motorcycle, you can legally travel the 25 miles from Goleta to Gaviota State Park, the beginning of the long, closed route around Point Conception. Afoot or on a bicycle, you become a trespasser as soon as you get to the end of Hollister Avenue in Goleta.

Hikers still face the problems we encountered when we

The march of February 25 was a long one, and it took the expedition to what Anza identified as the villages of Mexcaltitán, where again they were greeted with presents of large fish and sardines. The name Mexcaltitán survives today in tiny Mescal Island, southwest of Goleta.

Font judged the Indians gentle and friendly, but concluded it would not be easy to "reduce" them to the status of Christian converts because of the outrages inflicted on them by men presumed to be Christians.

Father Font was persuaded to say a short Mass on February 26. The march left the Goleta area at 8:15 in the morning, as he meticulously recorded, and continued until half past three in the afternoon to an Indian village called Rancheria Nueva, east of Point Conception. Font wrote of arroyos which ran inland "where there are seen many pines that bear good and large nuts, with shells so soft one can break them with the fingers."

Anza was well received by all Indians; the expedition was generously supplied with fresh fish.

It should be noted that along this pleasant channel coast Father Font made what may be history's first recording of California's future oil riches: ". . .Much tar which the sea throws up is found on the shores, sticking to the stones. Little balls of fresh tar are also found. Perhaps there are springs of it which flow out into the sea, because yesterday on the way an odor of it was perceptible. . . ."

first trespassed here in 1971. After crossing 101 and being blocked by the deadend of a short parallel road, we had to cross the highway again and start walking the railroad tracks, a definite act of trespass. After our first trespass, which had nothing to do with trying to follow the Anza trail of history, Thomas C. Buckley of Southern Pacific wrote to *Los Angeles* Magazine:

"Enjoyed Frank Riley's account, but a word of advice to those who might follow in his footsteps: Keep off the railroad right of way. This kind of trespassing can lead to death or serious injury. The only safe course is to stay well away from the tracks and, in particular, keep off railroad trestles or bridges where two serious accidents occurred within the past year in Northern California. . ."

Mr. Buckley was right, of course, as well kindly in his response to our trespass. We are not suggesting that you walk railroad tracks and trestles. There is another hazard today, and this is to railroad crews, passengers and trains: The madness of terrorism, the personal and political acts of violence so rampant in our world. The railroad tracks have to be protected from those who have put stones and other objects across them in deliberate efforts to derail a train. We trespassed on Southern Pacific right-of-way the first time, and I did so again, in order to make a point which also has to be made.

In walking the tracks out of Goleta, we soon encountered the kind of trestle that can be hazardous, a span several hundred feet above a deep canyon. After putting our inexpert ears to the rails, and deciding that no rail was approaching, we gingerly picked our way across. In another mile, we worked our way down a cliff to a grand, desolate beach. The tide was low enough to walk between the cliffs and the surf line, except at rocky points where we had to time the waves. We missed the last one, and had to wring out our clothing. After El Capitan Beach, an unmapped dirt road follows the top of the cliffs to El Refugio Beach. This is as far as we went along the coast in

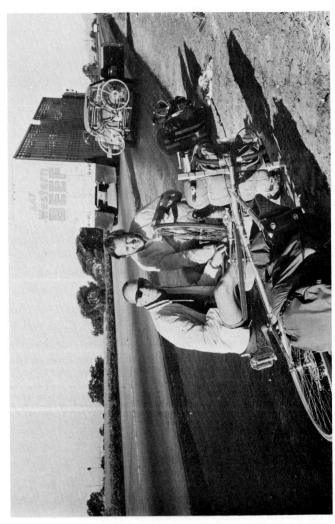

"...thrown off 101 by the Highway Patrol, two Mattel Toy Company employees bicycling to San Francisco had to come back on to take a chance of being arrested..."

1971, when we were not trying to follow the Anza trail—in fact, we didn't realize then that we were on a part of the trail. We turned inland at El Refugio, stayed for the night at Circle Bar B Ranch and next day climbed over the coastal range, down to Santa Ynez and Solvang.

Exploring, in 1975, the possibility of traveling by bicycle from Goleta to Gaviota, we almost immediately encountered two cyclists, employees of the Mattel Toy Company in Los Angeles. They were en route to San Francisco, and had been ordered off 101 by a Highway Patrol officer at the Hollister Avenue on-ramp. Finding, as we did, that there wasn't any other way to go, they had decided to return to 101 and take a chance on being arrested. We decided to take the same chance. Looking things over, it seemed that the officer had made a close judgement call. There are too off-turns for Highway 101 between Goleta and Gaviota to qualify as a freeway.

As we came closer to the multiplying problems of continuing to follow the Anza trail beyond Gaviota State Park, we had to make a decision either to give up on this part of the route or to do whatever was necessary to go on ahead. Our decision was to go ahead—not as a stunt or as defiance for the sake of defiance, but rather with the hope of being able to suggest some way to retrieve this highroad of history for our own and future generations.

Our first effort was a small subterfuge, which—again—we do not recommend. We stowed our bicycles on the bumper of our VW, stashed Zorba on the back seat and drove into Gaviota State Park one morning, looking—we hoped—like respectable motorists. So as not to compromise the Gaviota ranger, I waited in the parking area until his attention had been distracted—perhaps by Elfriede walking Zorba on a leash around his station. Then I scrambled up the 100-foot cliff to the railroad trestle that soars over the park. At the top, beside the tracks, a familiar white sign informed me of the illegalities I would be committing by

"Violators will be . . . . "

walking the railroad right of way. Anyone caught trespassing or loitering would be prosecuted under "369G-3691 or 555 Calif. P.C."

A picture window of Amtrak was clearly the only legal way to see from the land all the Point Conception route as Anza's people saw it. (We did this a few years ago in sybaritic fashion—a bedroom compartment with a double-bed beside the picture window for the all-day rail cruise between Los Angeles and San Francisco.)

Now, a few hundred yards down the track from the trestle bridge, there was a kind of magnificence to the loneliness. It was like creating a picture window and looking through it for the first time. Waves rolled against the base of cliffs far below. Wind made tracks across the brown dry grass. And there were access places down to bits of beach which likely hadn't been marked by a footprint for decades. You wondered if children in the Anza expedition had ever scrambled down to touch a toe in the water. Off on the horizon, a tanker moved up the coast—perhaps not too far from the wake of the sailing vessel that had transported Portolá and Father Serra to Monterey. The work road beside the tracks was comfortable for walking. The aloneness and the wind sweeping in, the clean breathing air and the sunlight on the sea would make you feel like running, and I did.

The only spooky sounds were the occasional popping and groaning of the railroad tracks; I couldn't hear a train coming so I thought the tracks must be expanding in the morning sun. Maybe so, but the thought made me more complacent than I would have been if Elfriede had been walking here with me. A Southern Pacific freight train, a trestle and I came unnecessarily close to coinciding at what in pre-Watergate days could have been called the same point in time.

I went on along the tracks until I got close to the outreach of Government Point at Cojo Bay, the area of Point Conception near where Anza had camped the first

"... you wondered if children of the Anza expedition ever scrambled down to touch a toe in the water ..."

night after leaving Goleta. The coastline turns sharply northward after Point Conception, then is breached by tiny Jalama Beach County Park, reachable from highway by 14 miles of Jalama Road. We had heard it was not feasible to go all the way along the railroad tracks from Gaviota State Park to Jalama County Park because of the likelihood of being arrested close to Jalama by security agents for a private ranch, who also were working with Southern Pacific to help police the railroad right of way. It had seemed plausible to us that if I turned back to Gaviota after reaching Government Point at Cojo Bay, we could then go on to Jalama County Park and try to complete another leg of the Anza trail by approaching Point Conception from the north.

If this all seems an enormously complicated effort to retrace an historical trail, that's precisely what it was—and would be for you. To clarify things a bit, take another look at the map of the Southern California coastline between Gaviota State Park and Jalama County Park. This coast is divided essentially between two vast ranches: The 14,440-acre Hollister Ranch controls nearly nine miles west of Gaviota to Point Conception; the 26,000-acre Bixby-Cojo Ranch is along the coast between Point Conception and Jalama.

As I was retracing my way along the Southern Pacific tracks, a passing pickup truck on a Hollister road slowed. I waved at the mustached young driver; he returned the wave and went on about his chores. I was carrying no pack and was wearing a light blue denim jacket and slacks; it probably seemed plausible that I had some right to be inspecting the Southern Pacific right of way.

Before going on to Jalama, we drove up to the gate of Hollister Ranch and were fortunate to meet Dick LaRue, General Manager. He was most gracious to us. We learned that the ranch had given permission for the Re-Enactment Committee riders from Santa Barbara to cross ranch property en route to the Bixby-Cojo Ranch and Lompoc, 113

Put your ear to the tracks to listen for a train.

an abbreviated version of Anza's trail around Point Conception; it had to be abbreviated because the next big piece of California real estate is currently occupied by Vandenberg Air Force Base. Dick LaRue has empathy with the re-enactment ride; he used to ride with the Anza caballeros out of Riverside.

At Hollister, we saw a centuries-old way of life in the process of transformation to a new form that seems to give hope for a small proposal of our own that had already begun to take form as I was walking along the Southern Pacific tracks. This Hollister land has indeed, as it claims, been virtually untouched since its Mexican land grant era, and for the past one hundred years has been a working ranch under single family ownership. Now it is divided into 135 parcels, each over 100 acres in size. The entire coastal frontage will be owned in common by the owners of the 135 parcels. Each parcel is selling for from $100,000 to $440,000. No parcel can be subdivided, and each is governed by deed restrictions that protect wildlife and nature in all its myriad forms. The concept is a harmony between man and his land—"an area of unequalled, unspoiled natural beauty under the strictest security and privacy." The beach area would forever be closed off to public access: "Each owner's enjoyment of his land and the sea can never be interrupted by intruders, motorbikes, firearms, congestion of people or organized activities."

The owner profile of the kind of people buying these $100,000-$440,000 "parcels" is not at all the mix you would expect. *Russell Lamb*, new owner of Parcel N. 43, lives on Hope Ranch in Santa Barbara; his business interests include a corporation in the Bahamas; the Hollister parcel will be the site of a second home. *Richard Vogel* is age 25. He and his wife *Jane* own and operate a commercial swordfishing boat out of Santa Barbara. They have purchased Parcel No. 18. Their interests also include growing cut flowers, and they have submitted to the Hollister Design Committee a plan for a growing area on

Some Indians came to the camp near Point Conception and offered to clean fish given to the colonists. Font tells this story:

"The Commander loaned to one of them his pocket knife, which had a silver handle and sheath. The Indian, who doubtless liked the knife better than his flint one, waited until nobody was looking, and then departed with it. Senor Anza afterward missed his knife, and calling another Indian who was there, told him to go to the village and say that unless they returned the knife he would have to go and punish them. The Indian went and a short time afterward returned with the knife, excusing the person who had carried it away, saying that he had taken it away innocently, thinking that it had been given to him, and that now he was afraid to return."

Anza accepted the explanation and considered the matter closed. Font had his own view: "This incident is proof of the inclination which every Indian has to steal."

So much fish was made available to the expedition that Anza had to leave some of it behind; his people couldn't carry any more, and didn't see the need to do so.

Father Font saw more than an inclination to thievery among the Channel Indians:

"Today, in exchange for glass beads, our people obtained at the villages several baskets and stone cups very well shaped, and wooden trays of various forms, and other curious pieces. I surmise that these Indians, who are so ingenious and so industrious, would become experts if they had teachers and suitable tools or implements, for they have nothing but flints, and with them and their steady industry they make their artifacts. . ."

Balancing it all out, Font concluded these Indians were prime prospects for a Mission.

their parcel. Parcel No. 80 is owned by a three-way partnership: *Dr. Walter Buettgenbach* and his wife *June* —he's a school administrator in the Palos Verdes area of Los Angeles; *Dr. Art McClean*—who is finishing his medical internship in San Francisco; *Jon and Clara Brough*—who have a commercial pottery business in Santa Barbara. One further example: *David Murray* graduated in psychology from the University of California at Santa Barbara. Finding no great demand for psychologists, he went to work for a landscape contractor from 1971-1973, and became interested in growing flowers and avocados along the coast. He acquired a real estate license, with a specialty in large agricultural properties. He's a musician who plays the piano with a jazz trio. His personal concern as a new owner of a Hollister parcel: "As the Ranch organization developes, it seems that more of us are realizing our on-going responsibility to help in that development and to cope with our shared problems and opportunities. For example, how best to use our commonly-owned property—the coastal strip, recreational areas and trails. The ocean teems with fish and shell life, but it's also extremely rich in kelp whose minerals include zinc so useful in enriching soil. We're considering best ways to harvest kelp along the beaches. . . ." The Bicentennial year of 1976 has been designated as the year when owners of the parcels, through various committees already functioning, "will take over and operate the Ranch entirely."

With this sort of information helping to germinate our thought for preserving the Point Conception part of the historic Anza trail, we went on to Jalama Beach County Park with the hope of being able to reach Point Conception from that direction.

At Jalama, the problems of re-tracing Anza's actual route looked thornier than ever. Adjoining the park immediately to the north is the vast territory of Vandenberg Air Force Base. The only access of Californians to the Vandenberg Coast is the road from Lompoc to the railroad   **117**

"...through early California..." on the way to Jalama

118

station whistlestop and beach enclave around Surf, some twenty miles north of Jalama. Bob Owens, Jalama Park ranger, formerly was in the Air Force at Vandenberg and subsequently worked for the Base. He reports to Military Police anyone starting out toward Surf along the Southern Pacific railroad right of way. Only a few weeks before our arrival, he reported three motorcyclists; they found the military awaiting them at Surf.

At the southern edge of the Park, we met Richard Weaver, a Bixby-Cojo security guard who patrols the area in a pickup truck. He is uniformed and armed. He also works closely with Southern Pacific to watch the tracks along the Bixby-Cojo Ranch. One of his worries is that "someone will put a rock on the railroad track some night and roll a freight train or an Amtrak passenger train right over into the Jalama campground." When I asked for permission to bicycle a ranch road back toward Point Conception, he referred me to Manager Lawrence Dutra, who lives on the ranch about two miles from Park headquarters. Dutra, a rugged, friendly man who would have fitted easily into the cast of *Bonanza*, interrupted his lunch to talk with us. He said that paperwork was in process at Bixby corporate offices in Los Angeles to permit the Re-enactment Committee riders to cross ranch property; one of the Committee organizers, Ruby Pico from Pico's Sporting Goods in Lompoc, had already been here to look over a route with him. On the back of one of his cards, Dutra wrote out permission to bicycle ranch roads toward Point Conception. (To save you and the Bixby-Cojo Ranch time-consuming phone calls and correspondence, I should stress the obvious: The kind of permit given to us and to the Anza trail riders would not normally be available to anyone wanting to travel this part of the Anza trail. But, again, the attitude we found at the ranch provided a small bit of additional hope for the proposal we were trying to formulate.)

119

Permission to trespass across Bixby-Cojo Ranch...

The ranch coastal road, separated by a fence on the landward side from the railroad tracks, is surfaced and easy to bicycle. So that's how, finally, I was able to photograph from the land the waves tossing spray against the rocky cliffs of Point Conception, which—as Father Font wrote—"is where the Santa Barbara Channel ends," and where "the road runs on top of the hills, for it is not possible to travel far on the beach because of the reefs." Looking northward today, Father Font would discern the Vandenberg satellite tracking station on a mountain outlined clear against the pale blue sky. As we left the ranch property, Security Officer Richard Weaver was waiting alongside the road to pick up our permit, politely and firmly.

From Jalama, we drove on to Surf with the bicycles again on our bumper. At Surf, not seeing any military folk around, I walked on down the railroad tracks toward Point Pedernales to view another section of the Anza route. I saw absolutely nothing of a military security nature.

Now, as to our proposal for a modest Anza trail around Point Conception:

The idea really comes from Keauhou Beach on the Kona Coast of the Big Island of Hawaii. Our friend Kenneth Emory of the Bishop Museum worked with a finally outraged public to promote tough new county regulations that would provide and protect public access to the Keauhou-Kona Coast. There must be a bicycling and walking path in perpetuity along the coast; all buildings and development must be set back far enough from the beach to allow for such a path, and developers are required to build it. However, after meeting people of manifest goodwill at the Hollister and Bixby-Cojo ranches, public outrage and eventual county or state action would not seem to be necessary in order to establish a quiet bicycle and walking path around Point Conception, thus permitting reasonable public access to what is after all a public resource: The coastline of California. The path could be closed to all motorized traffic. It could be kept separate

Point Conception as so rarely seen from the land.

from both ranch and railroad property. Public funding could provide for the relatively modest cost of building and maintaining the path; the ranches would perform a public service by donating a narrow strip of pathway to the state or county. Camping and ground fires would not be permitted along the Anza Pathway; nor would they be necessary, with Gaviota State Park and Jalama County Park at each end of the path. Park rangers could supervise access to the paths. We will bring this proposal to the attention of California's Governor Jerry Brown with the hope that public and private sector cooperation will follow. The beautifully crafted brochure prepared by the Hollister Ranch has this foreword: "There are those few places in the world where man can stand on verdant land and feel the sea and say, 'this is the land of man.' And there are those few men who can also say, 'this land is mine.'" The foreword needs but one more phrase: "And there are those few special places on earth which we all hold in trust for the family of man."

As for continuation of a similar Anza historical pathway across the lands held in trust by Vandenberg Air Force Base, two subsequent chapters will show there is ample precedent for such a path. With goodwill between the military and the public, a pathway could surely be worked out so as not to compromise national security.

Pending all this, we did work out an alternative to permit seeing part of the Point Conception coast by bicycle (or car), without breaking any laws. Gear up the Highway 101 grade from Gaviota for about four miles to the Highway 1 turnoff toward Lompoc. After another upgrade workout, you are on easy, rolling reaches of a surprisingly tranquil 20-mile bike ride into Lompoc. Take along a sleeping bag for an overnight detour along the way to Jalama Beach County Park. The 15 miles of Jalama Road are through early California ranch country. Jalama Beach Park is remote from the mainstream of traffic between Southern and Northern California, although 123

"At Punta de la Concepcíon," Font wrote, " the range which we have had on our right ends, and from this point the country sharply changes its appearance. All the land is thickly covered with flowers, and green with a great variety of grasses, good pasturage and fragrant and useful plants. Today from the time when we left camp, I saw much golden samphire, just the same in leaf and in taste as that grown on the rocks and on the walls along the coast of Cataluña. . . It was in full bloom, with yellow blossoms like small sunflowers, which were so abundant that they provided a very pleasing sight all the way. . ."

Salvador Ignacio was now two months old. Coyote Canyon seemed much longer ago than his birth on a Christmas Eve of snow and bitter cold.

Pedernales Point in 1776 was a village called Los Pedernales. Font found it somewhat poorer than the villages on the other side of Point Conception. A change in the weather may have influenced his viewpoint:

"All the forenoon the northwest wind was very strong and somewhat cold, with some fog, And then the wind turned to the north and the day was very dark, with a high fog that caused us a very cold and unpleasant afternoon . . . But the road is always in sight of the sea, and not very far from it. . ."

surfers know it well. The small park has 2,000 feet of beach and sand dunes, with fine surf fishing as well as surfing, and excellent prowling among rocks and fossils. You will get a sense of what the coast was like back in 1776. And you won't have to pack in food; the Park has a grocery store and snack bar. Returning to Highway 1, you'll skirt fields blanketed with flowers, all grown for seed. Since the distance from Jamala to Lompoc is only 20 miles, you'll have time to visit La Purisima Mission—not yet established as a way station for the Anza expedition— and to pedal out to Surf, where the expedition emerged from its long trek around Point Conception. You'll find Surf a fascinating little enclave, a train platform from another age for watching Amtrak thunder by, and on a weekend decidedly not tranquil. Dune cycles take over the beach; the waves are too wild for anyone except a skilled surfer.

Elfriede Riley on the beach at Jalama.

XII.
Lompoc to Pismo Beach

Highway 1 northward from Lompoc to Pismo Beach carries most of the traffic through this part of California. It skirts just to the east of Vandenberg Air Force Base. Unless you work on the Base, or are a student of maps, you wouldn't have reason to know that surface public roads cut across the heart of this military preserve. These roads are vital to the Vandenberg operation, and have never been a security hazard. They provide more than sufficient precedent for our proposed Anza pathway of history along the coast.

In lieu of such a pathway, you can approximate the Anza trail by traveling the Vandenberg roads. I pedalled them first in 1969, a time of the Vietnam tragedy when a bicycle rider with a mustache and longish hair got more than a passing glance from security patrols. Young GIs at the steering wheel of an officer's jeep would surreptitiously lift two fingers off the rim of the wheel to salute me with a sign of peace. Now young airmen could wave and grin without Vietnam in their future.

Turn up Floradale Avenue two miles west of downtown Lompoc. The avenue is in fact a country road across ploughed fields. It passes entrances to a U.S. "Correctional Institute" for military prisoners. A short distance beyond the Pine Canyon Entrance, Floradale ends at a Security

At four o'clock in the afternoon, the expedition made camp on the Santa Rosa River near the present railroad whistlestop called Surf.

"At six o'clock the next morning," Anza recorded, "I sent to learn the condition of the river. On account of the flood of water pouring into it by the tide of the sea, it was not fordable until half past twelve. . ."

Father Font must have slept in that morning to shake his chill from the weather of the previous day. February 29, 1776 is one of the few days of the entire march for which his diary does not begin with the same three words: "I said Mass."

When Father Font did get up, he apparently felt well enough to have recovered his natural curiosity. His description of Surf could be written today: "Sand dunes and sandy hills, and likewise a fairly wide flat area between two hills and half closed in by a pool of water which is there, having no exit toward the sea, but not very miry. In this flat, we saw a band of six bears. . . ."

Police Traffic Control and a public road marked S20, with wide shoulders in most stretches for safe bicycling. Three more miles take you to the Main Gate to Vandenberg facilities. You can rest in the parking area and watch the flow of traffic through the gate, which itself is three miles within the Base.

S20 turns northeast at the Main Gate to rejoin Highway 1. You continue on to the northwest and then north along Lompoc-Casmalia Road. It takes you by Utah Gate, the not-so-secret installation known as Vandenberg Air Force Base Golf Club, and then Titan Gate. Shortly before reaching the vicinity of the golf club, you pass a short piece of road leading to El Rancho Gate, not far from where Anza camped on San Antonio Creek. At the top of a grade three miles beyond Titan, you reach a closed entrance to Vandenberg Tracking Station. You see nothing of the station, or of the launching pads that send those awesome missiles arching across the sky toward Kwajalein Atol in the Micronesian Islands of the Central Pacific. It seems reasonable that an equally secure Anza pathway could be traced across Base territory.

You leave Vandenberg at the town of Casmalia, population about 200, "including the children." Casmalia is one of those priceless remnants of Western Americana that can so easily be missed with your foot on an accelerator instead of on a bicycle pedal or in a hiking boot. Traveling slow, we had the chance to inquire of a local citizen whether the town had any memorial to the Anza expedition. "Ask the Waterman," we were told. "He's been around Casmalia longer than anybody else —maybe his folks knew the Anzas . . . You'll find his house caty-corner across the road from the Hitching Post Restaurant. . . ."

It was the first time I'd ever talked to a Waterman. Bill Tognetti and wife sleep in the room where Bill was born 57 years ago. Bill was paralyzed by polio at age 4, but it didn't prevent him from taking over from his father as 129

The Waterman of Casmalia lives "caty-corner across the road from the Hitching Post . . ."

Waterman of Casmalia. Now his son is helping him read meters. The sequence of careers started, as Bill tells it, when O.C. Field developed the first oil refinery a half-mile from Casmalia. The refinery had a catch basin filled with water for floating off the oil. Townspeople from Casmalia would come with buckets to carry water back to their homes. Finally, O.C. said to Bill's father: "You get the people together. I'll furnish you the pipe to bring the water into town. Each house will have to pay to pipe the water in from the road. You put it all together, and it's your business. . ." Union Oil has since taken over from O.C. Field. Bill buys the water from Union and meters it out to 54 local households, at $6 per month. "There's not a whole lot of money in the business," he concedes. Casmalia learned about water conservation a long time ago: "We've always had to conserve—that's why you see no lawns. And if an hour or so goes by with no water—well, we're used to it. . ." Bill contends that the Hitching Post is one of the best barbecued steak places in California. But his folks didn't know the Anzas.

Black Road out of Casmalia takes you back to Highway 1. The "highway" into Guadalupe is a two-lane rural road through wide grazing pastures. We watched a train loaded with sugar beets pulling into Guadalupe's mustard-yellow station. Bud Wong's New York Restaurant is right on down the main street of this Mexican-American town. We hadn't stopped at Bud's place since we used it to pickup mail during our walk up the coast in 1971; I'd first stopped during the '69 bicycle trip. But traveling slow you have time to make friends. His lovely wife Toy was at the stove in the kitchen when I looked in after being away these long swift years. She came and put her arms around me and said, "Bud's dead." Bud was born here, and became Guadalupe's first Chinese city councilman, which says something warm about the people in this quiet back eddy of California. After going through high school in Santa Barbara and Curtis Wright Technical School in Los

Proceeding straight up the coast, generally following today's route of the Southern Pacific railroad, Anza was able to lead his expedition more directly from Surf to Pismo Beach than is possible by road for contemporary travelers. After a short day's march of only nine miles on the leap year day of February 29, camp was made at what he called Laguna Graciosa, at San Antonio Creek, Now Vandenberg Air Force Base territory. On the first day of March, the expedition kept a steady pace for almost ten hours, to El Buchón in Price Canyon, inland from Pismo Beach.

Father Font gives us the richness of detail that seldom appears in Anza's factual summaries:

"The village of El Buchón is so-called because when the first expedition of Senor Portolá came, there lived in this village a very high Indian chief called Buchón, famous in all the Channel for his valor and for the damage which he had done there with his wars.

"I learned that one of his principal wives still lived there, recognized by the heathen, who paid her tribute of a portion of their seeds; but he is now dead. Another of his concubines became a Christian and lives at the mission of San Luis, married to a soldier.

"This place has very fine water, and much firewood, which supplied us well. The beach which we followed on all this road is almost lacking in shells, and I saw very few there, although there were some rather rare and exquisite ones. I think this scarcity may be due to the fact that the sea is very wild on the coast and has very high tides."

Angeles, he went to Hong Kong to look for a wife. He came back to Guadalupe with Toy. That was in 1959. When I parked my bicycle outside and came in for lunch ten years later, their New York restaurant had a citation for "cuisine superieure and vin extraordinaire." Bud died of a heart attack early in 1975, while life was still young and full of happiness. Don't forget Toy when you pass this way; Bud Wong's New York Restaurant is still on the main street of Guadalupe.

Highway 1—Cabrillo Highway— continues northward out of Guadalupe. Within two miles, there's a turnoff across the fields to Oso Flaco Lake. After a soft sunset at the lake, we went on through Oceano and Grover City to Pismo Beach. Kon Tiki Inn, curved along the ocean, was new to us since our last visit. A thermal pool was between our patio and the beach. We simmered in it under the stars, and then went into dinner at a very good restaurant that unabashedly calls itself Trader Nicks. 59 miles, and a lot more, from Lompoc.

"... after a soft sunset on Oso Flaco Lake ..."

XIII.
Pismo Beach to Paso Robles

Under other circumstances of history, Pismo Beach could have become a Las Vegas on the central coast of California. In the 1920's legalized gambling briefly boomed Pismo.

When you are here on a quiet weekend, as we have usually been, you'll be grateful that the gamblers never did take over the town. And on a February Clam Festival Weekend, paying appropriate tribute to the famed Pismo Clam, you'll have action that couldn't be duplicated in Las Vegas. The Bicentennial year of 1976 also marked Pismo Beach's 30th Annual Clam Festival and Parade, with free clam chowder for one and all. Arts and crafts exhibits competed with a two and one-half hour parade, horse sprints on the beach, clam digging contests, hang gliders, hot-air balloonists, dixie and mariachi bands, dory boat races, barbecues, pancake breakfasts, Old West shootouts.

Since we were on the Anza trail a couple of months ahead of the festival, we left Kon Tiki in the calm of the early morning. By bicycle or horse, it's scarcely ten miles up Price Canyon, where Anza made camp, and into Mission San Luis Obispo de Toloso.

After five miles of canyon that widens into grazing land, turn northward on 227 through gentle farming country with a touch of country club.

By turning inland up Price Canyon to Mission San Luis Obispo, the Anza expedition departed from the original Portola road, which held close to the rugged coast northward. On this day, March 2, 1776, Anza permitted his diary to show more than the mere facts of the march:

"We arrived at the Mission of San Luis just as it was striking half past eleven, having traveled three and a half hours.

"The welcome which they gave us corresponded to their pleasure, and was such as may be imagined with people who spend all the days of their years without seeing any other faces than the twelve or thirteen to which most of these establishments are reduced, including the missionaries and the guard. And, aside from their long and painful exile from the world, as they say, we found them agitated by the event that happened at San Diego, thinking that after the first uprising another and worse one might have taken place. . .

"But having seen me, all melancholy and sadness disappeared, and they have turned to giving thanks to divine providence and to the present efficient government, that in such a timely manner this aid in the way of troops should have come to them."

It's intriguing to speculate what Father Font's reaction to the Mission might be today. The setting reflects a broad range of contemporary concerns. We found on the bulletin board a notice about the "mellow music and sweet harmony" concocted locally by Jacks Music Factory. Mission buildings are along green terraces of a stream where ivy overhangs benches. A picturesque footbridge crosses to a plaza that includes Wine Street Inn, Spindle Restaurant, Body Covers, Angie's Weed Nest and Sebastian's notable dinner house, offering steak, seafood, spirits. As of 1976, the old Mission has decided to make baptism a public affair: "Baptism isn't for the benefit of the child only. We have to enlarge upon the traditional idea of the sacrament as a kind of magic affair between the child and God. There is much more to baptism than this; the whole community is affected. The child is going to affect the community, and be affected by it. There should be a mutual understanding about that, and the community should be present in order to begin to get a realization of its part in the making of baptism, in bringing about the fulfillment of the baptism in the child, in helping the child fulfill its promises. . ."

San Luis Obispo astonishingly fulfills its promises to the traveler who travels slowly enough to come to a stop here. The start of the Bicentennial year was typical of most recent years. Cuesta College Auditorium presented an "Up with the People" concert. The San Francisco Opera Company was in town with "Marriage of Figuero." Art Center displayed "Four Women Etchers." The students at Cal Poly followed with Black Heritage Week, while Cuesta Auditorium punctuated its series of musical events with an evening "Creative Divorce Lecture."

On our various walks and bicycles treks through San Luis Obispo, we have at least tried to breakfast—if we couldn't overnight at Madonna Inn, the world's most outrageously rococo motel, where a banana on your breakfast cereal costs an extra $1.75, though coffee with

Mission San Luis Obispo was Father Font's dash of holy water. He approved of everything, from the natural setting to the Indians.

"This Mission," he wrote, "is situated in a beautiful site, on a small elevation near a stream of the finest water. It has very fertile lands and pretty fields. The Mission buildings consist of a large quadrilateral shed, with a square hall in the middle, and four rooms or divisions, one at each corner of the hall."

He especially approved of the way "the converted girls" were required to sleep "locked in." They were under the care of the wife of a soldier, "who is rather old and teaches them to sew and to keep clean." He added benignly: "They already do so very nicely, as if they were little Spaniards." No higher tribute could have come from the pen of this gentleman Spaniard from Catalonia. He found all the Indians "comelier and better featured than those of any other tribe" he had seen: "They are Indians with almost as good features as the Spaniards, and they are not so offensive to the smell as the other Indians."

Font's cup overflowed when Mass was turned over to him for Sunday, March 3. He was inspired to deliver a sermon on the theme of Transfiguration, comparing their hardship of the trail to the joy of resting at this "pretty Mission." But he did warn that this was but a transitory rest, such as Christ gave his disciples to prepare them "to suffer the trials which awaited them." After Mass, he baptized a seven-year-old Indian boy "whose Godfather was Commander Anza, the baptism being made with all the ceremony of the ringing of bells and the firing of muskets."

endless refills is only 25 cents. We have kind of an affair going on with Motel Inn, which can claim to be the world's first motel. Dr. Doris E. Ring, professor of history at North Carolina University, has documented this claim in her "Palaces of the Public, a History of American Hotels." She proves that the word motel "was first used in 1925 in connection with an establishment opened in San Luis Obispo, California." The establishment today is a pleasant complex of cottages, ivy arbors and a Steak House which our San Luis Obispo friends assert to be "the best restaurant in central California." The claim isn't easy to dispute. We were here on the evening of the Great Bull Buy, a once-a-year event. The selling is done by the agricultural department of Cal Poly, where students scientifically nuture bulls. The buyers are large cattlemen who pay an average of $1,000 for each bull. The prime bull of the day had just sold for $2,800. In such a milieu, a steak could not dare be less than superb.

We can document that it is legal, after the first two miles at least, to bicycle out of town on Freeway 101; there's no other way to bike northward to Anza's next camp near Atascadero. Turn off the freeway onto Highway 58 toward Santa Margarita. Bear left on the country road between the freeway and the Salinas River. Soon a sign will reassure you that this biking byway is indeed El Camino Real. Turn right on 41 across the bridge into Atascadero, then left on Templeton Road into an Old English countryside. Zig and zag along El Pomar and River Roads until you can cross the bridge to overnight at Paso Robles Inn. A non-strenuous 53-mile biking day from Pismo Beach, but you really do have to break it into two days by bivouacing for a night in San Luis Obispo.

"... in short, Mission San Luis de Toloso was Father Font's dash of holy water. ..."

XIV.
Paso Robles to King City

Just when you begin to wonder if following the Anza trail could possibly have any more discoveries, you come upon this section of the route between Paso Robles and King City.

For the cyclist, this should at least be a 2-day trip. It's a 62-mile bike ride from Paso Robles to King City without the 12-mile roundtrip between Jolon and San Antonio Mission—little more than an hour by car, but too long a bicycle day across these hills and mesas that can be as rugged as they are breathtakingly scenic. My 62-mile day in 1969 lasted from early morning to 9 P.M. And the detour to San Antonio, which I didn't make at that time, adds too much of interest to hurry along. After testing options this past autumn, we found it best to break the trip by camping overnight; there are excellent facilities along the shores of Naciemento and San Antonio reservoir lakes. Lake Naciemento Resort offers boat launching, hiking trails and fishing—plus all the camp amenities—at $4 per overnight.

The bicycle ride itself is too spectacular to hurry, even if you could hurry the hills. Follow 24th Street and Naciemento Lake Road out of Paso Robles. Orchards soften the hillsides of the curving mountain road. Naciemento Road—G14—is at first a long grade, and you

141

N

MONTEREY

SALINAS

CARMEL

LOS CORREROS

SALINAS RIVER

GONZALES

SOLEDAD

GREENFIELD

LOS OSITOS

KING CITY

SAN ANTONIO MISSION

JOLON

SAN ANTONIO

NACIEMENTO

ANZA'S ROUTE AS
IT WOULD LOOK TODAY:
ATASCADERO TO
MONTEREY

ATASCADERO

may want to do some walking and pushing. On the high mesa the road becomes gently undulating. You are riding a ridge between two lakes, San Antonio off to the right and Naciemento a shimmering mirror to your left. This is not the kind of mountain scenery you would expect to find in the coastal range of central California. The grade drops down to Bee Rock Store. As in 1969, Bee Rock still dispenses a long cool drink of orange juice. Continue on Interlake Road to Lockwood, where you pick up G14 again into Jolon. The road winds in a lovely and leisurely way between old trees and wide pastures. One expanse of grazing land had almost a thousand sheep, one little blacksheep among its white colleagues. You'll encounter more chipmunks than cars along this road, and far more cattle. Without realizing it, you phase into military reservation lands. No military reservation on earth could be approached with more tranquility, and the mood—amazingly—persists. Jolon itself is within Hunter Liggett Military Reservation, a ghost town with only a cafe to remind you that even the ghosts have long departed. Mission San Antonio is another six miles within the military reservation, on a road open to the public and marked with a memorial to the Anza expedition. If another precedent were needed, the example of Hunter Liggett shows what could be done for the Anza trail around Point Conception, and just as graciously.

For us, Hunter Liggett was altogether a new experience with a military reservation. The area is named for Lt. General Hunter Liggett, who commanded the 41st National Guard Division and later the First Corps of the American Expeditionary Forces during World War I, also serving as Chief of Staff for General Pershing. With 175,000 acres, and a use permit for another 92,000 from Los Padres National Forest, this is one of the largest military reservations in the United States, rising from gentle valleys to the often snow-capped summit of Mt. Junipero Serra, 5,862 feet above the Mission. The area is

Font got the Mass again on Monday morning, and the expedition didn't get off until almost nine o'clock, when he at last said "goodbye to my fellow countrymen, Father Caveller and his two companions, who were in every way very demonstrative."

The day's march lasted until five o'clock in the afternoon, over a spur of the Sierra de Santa Lucia, to camp at La Assumpción close to Atascadero. The following day was a long eight-hour trek to the first ford of San Antonio River. At four o'clock the following afternoon they reached Mission San Antonio.

"The welcome," Anza noted, "was as warm as at the foregoing missions. This one presented our troop with two very fat hogs and a supply of suet. . ."

used by the National Guard and reserve units of the Sixth Army.

Hunter Liggett realizes it is custodian for a great deal of historical treasure. The visitor receives a 10-page history of the lands within the reservation. It reflects considerable research, humor and social awareness. There is La Cueva Pintada, the Painted Cave, described as "a must for every visitor to Hunter Liggett." The walls are pianted with pictographs, the red coloring from deposits of cinnabar which in later centuries yielded a fortune in quicksilver. The cave apparently was central to the pre-Mission religious life of the Indians who lived around it in great numbers.

Dutton's Hotel once flourished in Old Jolon. The military historical summary observes in an un-military bit of musing: "If its adobe walls could speak, they could tell of many a romance that flourished, burst into bloom or died here." From the era of the Civil War, two powerful local families—the Duttons and the Tidballs—waged a magnificent feud that lasted for generations. Both families were Republicans and vied for the spoils when their party was in power. The Duttons, however, were canny enough to register one of their family as a Democrat, giving them control of the Post Office even when their own Republican candidate was defeated. A barometer of local political clout was always whether the Post Office was located in Dutton's Hotel or Tidball's Hotel. In its glory days, Jolon not only had two prestige hotels, but also three saloons, two blacksmith shops, two stores and a large dancehall featuring the music of Buckskin Bill Adams. Tiburcio Vasquez, described in the military account as a "sort of Robin Hood," turned the women of Jolon into groupies whenever he appeared on the dance floor. He robbed the Americanos and their stagecoaches with great flair, and shared his loot with poor Mexican and Indian families. A woman finally betrayed him, and when he was hanged, many a candle was burned at the altars of Mission San Antonio.

On the high road through Lake Naciemento country: "...one of the state's most scenic mountain routes..."

146

Along the six miles of open road from the ghosts of Jolon to the Mission and military headquarters, you share the road with range cattle as well as jeeps. Then, there it is—crowning a rise of a hill—what appears to be the unholy wedding between California mission architecutre and a Byzantine mosque with a golden dome. We thought, as do most first-time visitors, that we were gazing upon Mission San Antonio. But don't blame it on Father Serra; the Mission is a half mile on down the road. What you are seeing isn't a mirage, either. It's the *other* Hearst Castle, the one virtually unknown to present generations of Californians and California visitors. William Randolph Hearst built what he called his Hacienda during 1929-30, when something of a Depression was under way elsewhere. The plans were drawn by Julia Morgan of San Francisco, regarded as one of the first women to be nationally recognized as an architect. The gold dome has to be authentic William Randolph. Western artist William Runyan was engaged to do the murals and paintings that still adorn Hacienda walls. This was a working ranch as well as a play place. Ten thousand acres were tilled around it; thousands of cattle grazed the hills. Of course, Marion Davies was here, too—along with such frequent party guests as Arthur Brisbane, Louella Parsons, William Powell. The military account of those days soars off again into what is definitely not Pentagon prose: "Many a colorful and exciting party has been staged in the Hacienda to the accompaniment of lively music, the tinkle of glasses and the lilting laughter of lovely ladies."

In 1940, the military needed another reservation for what would soon be World War II. The U.S. Government purchased all of the lands of today's reservation, seventy-five percent of which were owned by William Randolph Hearst, for $2.2 million. It was quite a buy. The Hacienda alone, now military headquarters, has to be worth as much as the original purchase price. Visiting generals stay overnight beneath the golden dome of the Tower Room; 147

That other Hearst Castle: ". . .an unholy wedding between California mission architecture and a Byzantine mosk with a gold dome. . ."

Hunter Liggett's commander occupies the suite just below. Visitors who come down the road from Jolon are made welcome. The roads being unfenced, we found a black cow standing sentry duty at the gate. Except in the busiest of training times, someone is available to give you a tour of the Hacienda. You can stay for a moderately priced lunch or dinner, but have to be a guest of an officer in order to overnight.

On down the road at the third Mission founded by Father Junipero Serra, Brother Timothy was getting together his costume to play the part of Father Font while riding a donkey with the Anza re-enactment committee riders. He was also trying to find time just to sit on a donkey so he wouldn't get too saddle sore during the two-day ride. Brother Timothy agreed that Father Font might not have been happy about riding a donkey, although he too was a Franciscan and St. Francis urged donkey riding for humility. What would the injunction of St. Francis be today? Brother Timothy felt it might be: "Thou shalt not ride about thy parish in a Rolls."

Brother Timothy and Father Joe are alone at the Mission. Sometimes they come close to outnumbering their parishioners at a Sunday Mass; Jolon isn't exactly a population base for a parish, and in peacetime everybody in the military who can get away prefers to go home for the weekend. But the two padres don't have time for riding around in a Rolls or any other vehicle. They are continuing to rebuild the Mission quite literally with their own hands.

Early in the 19th century, Mission San Antonio was a self-contained city. Thousands of Indians were at work in animal husbandry, orchards, vineyards, metal forges, shoe shops, lumbering, soap-making, candle-making, carving and painting. When Mexico became independent, the Indians of Mission San Antonio participated in the voting for a delegate to be sent to the new Congress in Mexico City. The Franciscans had always intended, Brother Timothy

ON MARCH 6,1776 CAPTAIN JUAN
BAUTISTA DE ANZA ARRIVED AT THIS
MISSION ON HIS FAMOUS OVERLAND
EXPEDITION FROM SONORA, MEXICO,
TO MONTEREY AND SAN FRANCISCO.
HE WAS ACCOMPANIED BY 240 COLONI-
NISTS & THE DIARIST, PADRE PEDRO
FONT, WHO WROTE "THE INDIANS OF
THIS MISSION ARE TOTALLY DISTINCT
FROM THOSE I HAVE HITHERTO SEEN."
HE RECORDED THE PLACE AS "MISSION
SAN ANTONIO IN THE VALLEY OF
THE OAKS."

Approaching Mission San Antonia: On a part of the Anza trail you can *follow across a military reservation.*

believes, to return the lands to the Indians when the time was right and move on to "new spiritual conquests." Secularization was ordered by Mexico City before the Franciscans felt the time was right. Then the U.S. took over California, "and the Indians were forever deprived of the lands that rightfully belonged to them."

By the end of the 19th century, Mission San Antonio was more of a ghost town than Jolon is today. There hadn't been a padre since 1882. Ranchers had helped themselves to timber and tiles. In 1928, the Franciscans were asked to take over the ruins. Another two decades went by before they had any funds to start rebuilding. In 1949, the Hearst Foundation got things going with a grant of $50,000. Brother Timothy came here the next year, virtually right out of seminary. He's been involved in the reconstruction ever since then. Old pictures were available, so the restoration could be completely authentic. Soon archaeological digs will begin to learn more about the Indian civilization that preceded the Mission. Bicentennial preparations intruded on all this, but Brother Timothy didn't mind: "In the east, we are commemorating battle-fields. Here we celebrate the coming of men and women and children peacefully into a new land. And can you conceive what an enormous reassurance it was for the Indians to be confronted with visual evidence that there were Spanish soldiers who actually had *wives*? Up to the arrival of the Anza expedition, the padres had been trying to use a painting of the Virgin Mary as evidence of family life in the white man's world, and she wasn't always convincing—not with the way the soldiers acted toward Indian women. . . . . ."

Of all the Missions, San Antonio—by the grace of Hearst and the U.S. military—is set in surroundings least changed since Anza's day. Brother Timothy wasn't alarmed that some 10,000 visitors expected at Bicentennial festivities for the Anza re-enactment would bring changes by suddenly re-introducing Mission San Antonio via late 20th

Font found the construction of Mission San Antonio "to be better than that of the others, "with fine conveniences and advantages." But he didn't like the some 500 Christian Indians. For a man of the cloth, he had a ready eye for the comparative attractiveness of Indian women, and noted that these were no where near the standard of San Luis Obispo, and that they "do not bang their hair, as I have said of those of the Channel and at St. Luis." He rated the men as "degenerate and ugly," and the local language as "barbarous and ridiculous crackling and whistling and gutteral sounds." He lamented: "There is no thorn of grief which more torments the heart of a minister who desires to serve God in the ministry of the conversion of souls, nor any harder toil, than to find himself among people of such diverse and barbarous languages. . . ." But he did get the Mass, and "afterward I assisted with my musical instrument in another Mass, which we sang with all possible solemnity. . . ."

A Lieutenant who had stayed behind at San Gabriel to look for some deserters now caught up with the expedition, and Font got quickly to the nitty gritty of what had happened. "The Corporal of the Guard of San Gabriel had fallen in love with a woman of our expedition while we were in San Diego, and since he had nothing to give her as a means of getting into her good graces, he urged the muleteers to give him something of what was in their charge, chocolate and things." One theft led to another, and finally all concerned decided to flee.

century television. How could there be too much change within a military reservation? He joked with us in his wry way about California's Governor Jerry Brown having been trained so austerely by the Jesuits, but he hoped the Governor also would be on hand: "Jerry's busy breaking molds, but maybe he can find time to visit us. His father did. . . ."

When you are eventually able to leave the old-new world cloistered within Hunter Liggett Military Reservation, bicycle on down Jolon Road—G14 again—to King City.

"...Mission San Antonio — by grace of Hearst and the military — is set in surroundings least changed since Anza's day..."

XV.
King City to Monterey

After Brother Timothy and William Randolph Hearst's other castle, the next day will be a quiet one for reflection—and trying to fit yourself into the mood of how Anza's people felt at finally approaching Monterey.

It can be a surprisingly reflective approach, even today—for both the motorist and the cyclist. We found it best to stay just west of the Salinas River all the way, as Anza did most of the way. Getting out of King City therefore requires somewhat more maneuvering than was necessary for the Anza expedition.

Swing off onto Central Avenue just north of King City and pedal on to the Greenfield-Arroyo Seco Road. Detour west to the junction with G17—Seco Road. Near Soledad, Seco Road becomes Fort Romie Road and then River Road, but it's G17 all the way, and a real treasure of a bicycle road. You are pedalling through the sugarbeet fields of Salinas Valley. Salinas River keeps appearing off to your immediate right as bits of a silver ribbon in the sunlight. About half way to Spreckels, you pass close to the Anza campsite near Chualar. At Spreckels, turn south and circle along Fort Old Military Reservation on Monterey-Salinas Highway 68 for the last ten miles into Monterey. This is a busier road and has to be followed more alertly.

155

From Mission San Antonio, the expedition went on to camp at Los Ositos, between King City and Greenfield. On the next morning of March 9, Father Font was pushed to hurry his Mass so that the march could get going by eight o'clock. They followed the Salinas River all day to the next camp close to Chualar. From here they followed the river to a point very near Spreckels, then took the route of the present highway into Monterey. They reached the Presidio of Monterey in heavy rain. Anza looked back for a moment in his diary for that day:

"From the time of leaving my Presidio in Tubac until my arrival here, sixty-two days of marches have been made, this being a few less than I estimated even when I was in Mexico. In all these days of travel, we have had no losses among the people whom I have conducted except the woman mentioned as having died of childbirth on the first night after we set forth. Other adversities experienced and related herein are those common to roads less extended and more open, and even provided with everything necessary to guard against mishaps. The rain storm continued until nightfall."

As you enter Monterey, three volleys of artillery are not likely to be fired, but you can chant your own personal *Te Deum.*

Helen Shropshire, who originated the idea for the Anza Re-Enactment Committee, has also devoted—as we noted earlier—much of her time in volunteer work for California Heritage Guides, headquartered at 181 Pacific Street in Monterey. Let the Heritage Guides guide you through more than a Bicentennial of history around the Monterey Peninsula. They will tell you that "the best way to explore Old Monterey is on foot." They have mapped out a series of leisurely 1½-hour walks introducing you to the streets of history around Robert Louis Stevenson's home and the old Presidio Chapel; to Cannery Row not quite as it was for John Steinbeck; to Custom House Plaza area where 600,000 square miles of the west were officially proclaimed to be U.S. territory. There are places along all the walks for sitting in a still secluded garden, for browsing an art gallery and for coming upon a Mexican restaurant you can forever after claim as your own discovery.

We have a walk of our own to share that may bring you closest to 1776. The millions of viewers who follow the Crosby golf tournament on TV, and catch glimpses of the Monterey Peninsula in segments of fairway or over-the-water action, may not realize that the 17-mile Drive around the Peninsula isn't necessarily for driving—either with a golf club or an automobile. It is in reality best for hiking, biking or crisscrossing on horseback trails. You can save the $3 automobile entrance fee by walking or pushing your bicycle through one of the four gateways into the 5,400-acre Del Monte preserve. We first discovered that the 17-mile drive was for walking four summers ago, during our Los Angeles-San Francisco walk. We had to cut across the Del Monte properties in order to proceed afoot from Carmel to Monterey. This means turning to the right after you get through Carmel Gate off Ocean Avenue and heading uphill. It's still the best way to begin walking the

The Royal Presidio of Monterey was not exceedingly royal on March 10, 1776, but the welcome was more than joyful. Three volleys of artillery were fired to salute the success of a truly unparalleled expedition. Yet that evening Father Font was moved to write with customary candor:

"This is a very small affair, and for lack of houses people live in great discomfort. Nor is this for want of materials, but for lack of effort directed to the purpose. The Commander, indeed, had to lodge in the storehouse, and I in this dirty little room full of lime, while the rest of the people accomodated themselves in the plaza with their tents as best they might."

After such a night, things could only get better for Father Font, and they did the next morning with the arrival of Father Junipero Serra and four other friars from Carmel Mission:

"Great and very special was the joy which we all felt on our arrival, and after we had saluted each other with many demonstrations of affection it was arranged to go and sing the Mass.

"We sang the Mass, then, as an act of thanksgiving for our successful arrival, I sang it again at the altar, and the five fathers assisted me, singing very melodiously and with the greatest solemnity possible, the troops of the presidio and of the expedition assisting with repeated salvos and volleys of musketry, all this together causing tears of joy to flow. . ."

entire 17-mile drive because it saves the intimacy of the
ocean shoreline until the second half of the hike. Carry a
light knapsack with a picnic lunch. Also a warm sweater
and a poncho, for the weather can change as swiftly for
you as it often did for Father Font.

Each interest point is numbered on the map you get at
the gate. Shepherd Knoll is No. 1. It looks down into the
azure bay first sighted by the amazing Portuguese navi-
gator Cabrillo in 1542. More than a Bicentennial later,
Portolá and Father Serra arrived in this same bay to found
the Carmel Mission. You've walked 9.6 miles by the time
you get down to Spanish Bay. The serenity of the calm
blue waters can be deceptive. It was here that the wreck of
the Roderick Dhu happened in 1909.

Continue on another mile for your picnic lunch at Point
Joe, overlooking the restless sea. It's one of the few places
in the world where so many currents meet. I like the story
of Joe, for whom the point is named. He did something for
the squatters of the world. An old Japanese squatter, he
successfully fought off every attempt to evict him from
the panorama of golf courses and neo-Renaissance estates.
The Del Monte Corporation finally conceded his squatter's
rights and bought him off for cash.

The bike trail coming in from Pacific Grove ends just on
down the road near Seal and Bird Rocks, haunt of
immense flocks of sea gulls, black carmorants and sea
ducks. Sea lions loll around them.

The road loops off the main drive to entice you to
Cypress Point, perhaps the finest lookout on the Peninsula.
Walk off the road again through the oldest grove of
Monterey Cypress in existence. Another half mile brings
you to the footpath leading out to the Lone Cypress, the
world's most photographed tree. Its improbable survival
had come to epitomize the struggle of all nature forms
against extinction.

Pescadero Point comes to life when you have time to sit
and think about Maria del Carmen, a widow who must

159

Amid such a flowing of joyful tears, the great Father Serra added the ultimate touch by deferring for the sermon to Father Font, who had already sung his way through two Masses. It was one of the great moments, if not the greatest moment, of Font's life, and he was not unprepared for it:

"I took as a theme *Simile est regnum caelorum sagenae missae in mare, et ex omni genere piscium congreganti:* 'Thy Kingdom of Heaven is like onto a net which He casts into the sea with which are caught all kinds of fish.' "

From this springboard, Font reprised again the entire march from San Miguel to Tubac and on to California and Monterey: ". . .We entered the heathendom of the two rivers, the Gila and the Colorado, with the same confidence and security as if we were entering the lands of Christians, and we forded the formidable Colorado without the least mishap." This was no moment for remembering the heathen who had held him on his horse. His mellifluous voice rolled on: "We crossed the sand dunes through which the Indians scarcely dare to pass because it is a land so bad that not even birds inhabit it. . ." The blizzards of Coyote Canyon were then put in new perspective by the fervor of his oratory: "Might we not have died, just as so many animals died of cold? But why do I say die? Nobody even became ill. . ."

Father Font hit the high notes of his peroration with words that must have surprised many, maybe himself as he later recorded them so faithfully in his diary: ". . .And I, in the name of God and of the King of our Lord, give thanks to our Commander, Don Juan Bautista de Anza, for the patience, prudence and good conduct which as chief he has shown in commanding this expedition, and I promise him that God will reward him for his labors."

have been kin to the merry widow who so often plagued Father Font. Maria acquired most of the peninsula when her husband died in 1841. It was a land grant rancho, but—as one historian puts it delicately—Maria was "by nature neither rancher nor widow." She sold the peninsula to get a townhouse with latticed windows in Monterey, then blithely sold it again to David Jacks of Monterey. Jacks subsequently unloaded the land for $5 an acre on San Francisco's Big Four—Charles Crocker, Leland Stanford, Mark Hopkins and Collis P. Huntington. It's a joy to speculate who would own all these golf courses if an heir of Maria's first buyer ever showed up.

Even if you have to wait around Monterey as long as Anza's colonists did, you won't find time heavy on your hands. And if you're a hiker or biker who likes to spend a night in a way Maria del Carmen would have savored, try the sybaritic comforts of fairway accommodations for two at Del Monte Lodge.

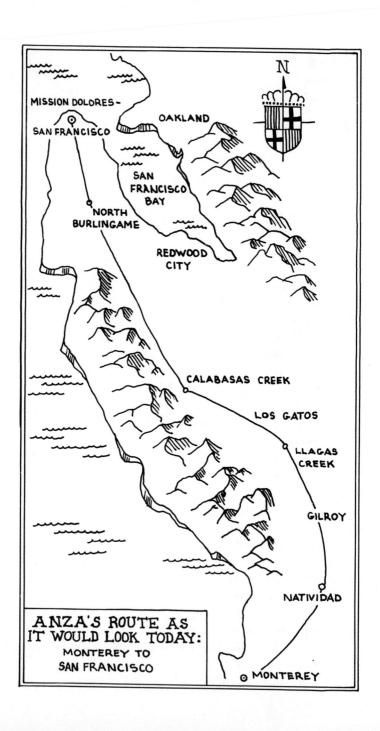

N

MISSION DOLORES –
SAN FRANCISCO

OAKLAND

SAN
FRANCISCO
BAY

NORTH
BURLINGAME

REDWOOD
CITY

CALABASAS CREEK

LOS GATOS

LLAGAS
CREEK

GILROY

NATIVIDAD

ANZA'S ROUTE AS
IT WOULD LOOK TODAY:
MONTEREY TO
SAN FRANCISCO

MONTEREY

XVI.
"Harbor of Harbors"

If you have ever had a love affair with or in San
Francisco—and who hasn't?—a reading of Father Font's
diary will prove this could happen just as easily in 1776 as
in 1976. Nob Hill, the Powell Street cable car, North
Beach, the hills a shimmering translucence at night and
Golden Gate Bridge misty in the early morning didn't seem
at all necessary to set the mood.

Font called San Francisco "a marvel of nature—harbor
of harbors." He wrote of his vista from what is now Fort
Point, and perhaps should be Font Point:

"We ascended a small hill and then entered upon a mesa
that was very green and flower-covered, with an abundance
of violets.

"This mesa affords a most delightful view, for from it
one sees a large part of the port and its islands, as far as the
other side, the mouth of the harbor, and of the sea all that
the sight can take in as far as beyond the farallones.
Indeed, although in my travels I have seen very good sites
and beautiful country, I have seen none which pleased me
so much as this. And I think that if it could be well settled
like Europe there would not be anything more beautiful in
all the world, for it has the best advantages for founding in
it a most beautiful city. . ."

Herb Caen in 1776 might have used the same words.   163

But after all his work and dreams, Juan Bautista de Anza was not actually to found here what Father Font could envision as a most beautiful city. From the moment of the expedition's arrival in Monterey, Anza began to be enmeshed in the web of intrigue and rumors woven by Captain Commander Rivera, who was still in San Diego. The colonists were told how miserable were conditions in the San Francisco area. Their livestock was virtually impounded in a stockade for reasons of "security." Anza had orders from the Viceroy, but Rivera was Captain Commander of all Alta California and communications with Mexico City could take a year or more. Anza sent off a letter to Rivera in San Diego, then became ill himself for several days with a severe pain in his groin, which no one on this far frontier could then diagnose. When he recovered, he determined to explore San Francisco with the soldiers from Tubac who were to remain under his personal command. The padres of the Mission were all on his side, for Rivera had also walled them off from establishing a San Francisco Mission. They had come to believe their Captain Commander was a wily and not always rational man.

At 9:30 on the morning of March 23, 1776, Anza, Father Font, Lieutenant Moraga, eight soldiers from Tubac and three from Monterey who had been persuaded to go along as guides, set off for San Francisco, carrying provisions for twenty days. They stayed west of the present road to Salinas, and camped at today's Natividad after covering about 21 miles. The second day took them west of Gilroy to Llagas Creek. The Indians, Font wrote "offered us some of their game, and the Commander accepted a rabbit and an arrow which they offered him as a sign of peace." From Llagas, they proceeded northwest to the pass at Coyote, then camped near Cupertino on Calabasas Creek, On March 26, they passed a tall redwood tree that would still be standing in the 20th century at Palo Alto and camped in North Burlingame. They rode on next day past Millbrae, San Bruno and—according to Font's meticulous diary—apparently veered seaward to pass between sand dunes on their left and Lake Merced on their right. They then crossed Golden Gate Park to camp on Mountain Lake a mile and a half south of Fort Point, at the southern edge of the present Presidio Military Reservation. On the morning of March 28, Font said Mass at Fort Point. Anza erected a Cross for him there, and under stones at the base buried a notice of their exploration. Font had a chance to come on again after Mass for the blessing of the Cross, and was already in a state of pure euphoria when he ascended the small hill to write his love letter to San Francisco.

Turning back to explore the other side of the bay beyond Oakland, Berkeley and Richmond, they first passed Dolores Creek south and west of Fort Point. Font found the area fragrant with wild violets, and concluded that a Mission should be established there. They probed eastward from the East Bay to Antioch and almost to Tracy, then headed southward to the Salinas River and Monterey.

Anza's people at Monterey were overjoyed to learn that their future homeland in San Francisco was not the desolate and hostile region depicted by Rivera. Finding no response to his letter to Rivera, Anza decided to try to resolve things by meeting with the Captain Commander in Southern California—or, failing that, to return to Mexico City and there try to break the impasse. He left the expedition under the command of Lieutenant Moraga, and started south with Father Font and his own Tubac soldiers.

The people wept as Anza left them. For the first time, this strongly self-disciplined son of the frontier permitted the barest glimpse of his own heartache to be reflected in his terse diary:

"This day has been the saddest one experienced by this presidio since its founding. When I mounted my horse in   165 the plaza, the people whom I have led from their fatherlands, to which I am returning, remembering the good or bad treatment which they have experienced at my hands, came to me sobbing with tears, which they declared they were shedding more because of my departure than of their exile, filling me with compassion. They showered me with embraces, best wishes and praises which I do not merit. . . ."

Thus it was that Lieutenant Jose Joaquin Moraga was in the command position when the expedition finally started for San Francisco on June 17. They remained for a month at the Dolores Mission site picked by Father Font—while on the other side of the continent, unknown to them, a Declaration of Independence was being proclaimed with the ringing of the Liberty Bell at Philadelphia. The Presidio of San Francisco was officially founded on September 17, 1776. The San Carlos was in port. Its officers and crew stood with the colonists. Four padres said Mass. At its conclusion, Father Palóu recorded, "All sang *Te Deum Laudamus*, accompanied by peals of bells and repeated salvos of cannon, muskets and guns, and the San Carlos responded with its swivel guns. . . ."

Not the least of the difficulties caused by Rivera was the problem of celebrating multiple arrival dates a Bicentennial later. The San Francisco committee decided, in effect, on two celebrations. The first would begin March 27, when Anza's exploratory arrival in San Francisco County would be re-enacted by riders arriving along the beach from San Mateo County. They would camp two nights at Mountain Lake, and repeat the raising of the Cross ceremony on March 28. The U.S. Army would provide military escorts within the Presidio. On June 26, the arrival at Mission Dolores and the subsequent founding of the Presidio would be telescoped into one commemoration with prayers, hymns and a fiesta on the Presidio parade ground.

There are some interesting options in retracing the route today, by walking or bicycling, from Monterey to San

Francisco. After testing several, the following is our recommendation:

From Carmel Hill Gate along the 17-mile Drive, take Highway 1 briefly to Munras Road. Follow Munras, Abrego, Fremont and El Estero into Del Monte, and then along the bikeway through Fort Ord. Out of Marina, ride Highway 1 to the quiet Molero Road loop through artichoke fields. The loop will bring you into Highway 1 below Moss Landing, a quaint fishing village for lunch in spite of the shadow of the P.G.&E. generating plant. Leave Highway 1 again to follow Salinas Road toward Pajaro and Watsonville. A gentle day of about 35 miles. We stayed overnight in the pleasant ambience of El Rancho Motel, across from the 18th hole of the Pajaro Valley Golf Club.

At Watsonville, a decision has to be made. After crossing Pajaro Creek, Anza kept eastward of the hills and west of Gilroy. For the cyclist, the easiest route to Gilroy is along Riverside Drive—Highway 129, generally following the Pajaro River. This, however, means challenging the Highway Patrol along 101 into Gilroy. A shorter, more scenic, though initially more difficult route is to follow the road marked 152 over Mt. Madonna County Park on the way to Gilroy. For the non-purist, this means pushing your bicycle slowly up the hairpins of Hecker Pass. Before reaching Gilroy, turn north on G8-Watsonville Road. Watch for the turn northwestward along Uvas Road and Uvas Lake reservoir. This is now the route of my 1969 bicycle ride from San Francisco to Los Angeles. As you can see from your county map, it is not at all as circuitous as it sounds. It will show you the countryside most nearly as it was described by Father Font. Stay on Uvas Road through ranching country to Calero Lake reservoir. G8 turns more westward here on McKean Road into Almaden Road just below San Jose.

With some ingenuity, and a willingness to pedal and push a grade here and there, it is quite possible to follow the Anza route between San Jose and San Francisco with as much tranquility as we found so unexpectedly across the Los Angeles metropolitan area. Head west off Almaden Road into Blossom Hill Road. Let Winchester, Campbell, Prospect and Stelling Roads circle you around Cupertino. Fremont, Miramonte, Cuesta and Fremont again lead into Junipero Serra Boulevard, which becomes Alameda de las Pulgas. If these sound like strange-sounding roads to pursue in getting to San Francisco, be consoled that you won't have to contend with Bayshore Freeway traffic. And we are presuming that you won't be in a hurry while following these last miles of the long Anza trail. You'll be grateful for a night's rest at Howard Johnson's on Stevens Creek Blvd. in Cupertino.

Alameda de las Pulbas will get you almost to San Mateo, where you can take Hayne Road up to the Junipero Serra-280 Freeway. A small road parallels it to Trousdale Drive. Challenge the freeway very briefly to the Skyline Boulevard turnoff just beyond Milbrae. Skyline will take you into San Francisco County between Lake Merced and the sea. Follow Great Highway through the western edge of Golden Gate Park, then eastward on Fort Lobos toward the Presidio of San Francisco.

We here want to pay tribute to two unique publications which turned us on to very special walking and bicycle routes in and around the Presidio area. *Bicentennial Bike Tours*, covering routes all over the U.S., was put together by Gousha Publications of San Jose with the assistance of the League of American Wheelman. Their 25-mile route from Mission Dolores around the Presidio, through Golden Gate Park and around Lake Merced was designed for "San Francisco's 200-year-old Spanish beginnings." It proved to be a jewel, and we commend it to you. Our colleague Margo Patterson Doss, widely known for her weekly walk column in the *San Francisco Chronicle*, has written—often poetically—*Paths of Gold*, published by Chronicle Books. One of her paths is the Presidio History Trail. She tells you: "Look for the stone marker on the south side of

Mountain Lake which marks the site where Captain Juan Bautista de Anza, Lieutenant Moraga, Father Font and their party camped in 1776." She also tells you about a military procedure that establishes still another precedent for our proposed Anza Pathway around Point Conception: "Begin by signing in at the Military Police Station, at the corner of Lincoln and O'Reilly, about three blocks inside the Lombard Street Gate . . . On registration, the Sergeant at the desk will issue a guide map to the historic trail, which delineates the route with arrows and describes the 28 stops along the way. . ."

For the greater part of two centuries, Juan Bautista de Anza was remembered with few such courtesies along any of the trails he blazed across the west, before and after the expedition to San Francisco.

During the decade after the arrival at Monterey, his star was bright. He became Governor of New Mexico, where his military skill and his known friendships with the Indians turned the tide of the disasterous frontier wars. In 1786, the year of the Virginia statute, Anza and the Comanche leader Ecueracapa embraced, and New Mexico entered upon a generation of relative security and unprecedented growth. He crossed trails again in New Mexico with the almost unbelievable Father Garcés, who hiked there alone from the Pacific coast while the frontier was still seething.

At the Yuma crossing of the trail to California, the explosion of outrage which Father Serra had long predicted finally occurred. One village too many had been looted by passing troops and muleteers; one Indian woman too many had been raped. Chief Palma, who had embraced Anza, tried to contain the uprising, but was swept along by his own people. Father Garcés had returned to the Yuma nation. Palma tried to save his life by urging that he be brought before a tribunal, but he had to watch this loving and incredibly heroic priest, who had shared a thousand campfires with the Indians, be clubbed to death. Paradoxically, Garcés went to death with Captain Rivera.

169

The Yuma road was closed. Officials who had been warned for more than a decade of what would happen began adroitly to turn the criticism toward Anza. Why had he established the overland route through the territory of such a powerful and dangerous Indian nation?

Life was full, but not often long on the frontier. Juan Bautista de Anza died in obscurity and disgrace in 1788, at age 52. Father Font was not there to speak a word for his old commander; Fray Pedro Font, gentleman priest from Catalonia, had lived out his allotted years at age 43. Anza's body lay beneath the floor of a Jesuit church at Arispe, Sonora, until 1963, when it was exhumed and identified by historical researchers funded by the University of California. The government of Mexico commissioned a statue showing him astride a spirited horse. It stands at Hermosillo, capital of Sonora. Another was given to the city of San Francisco.

When you follow his trail quietly and slowly, as we have been privileged to do, you know that though the statue may honor him, it cannot alone tell his story.